Complicated Grief

D1473925

ALSO BY LAURA MULLEN

Complicated Grief

Laura Mullen

SOLID OBJECTS

NEW YORK

Grateful acknowledgment is made to the editors of the following journals and anthologies in which these works (in slightly differing forms) first appeared: *American Book Review*, *Black Ice*, *Civil Disobediences*, *(Dzanc's) Best of the Web 2009*, *Eleven More American Women Poets in the 21st Century*, *The Fairy Tale Review*, *The Iowa Review*, *Paraspheres*, *Ploughshares*, *Tarpaulin Sky*, and *Versal*. The author is grateful for the support of the Louisiana Board of Regents through the Board of Regents Support Fund: contract number LEQSF (2012-13)-RD-ATL-03.

Design by Erik Rieselbach

Printed in the United States of America

Cloth
ISBN-10: 0-9862355-1-2
ISBN-13: 978-0-9862355-1-1

Paper
ISBN-10: 0-9844142-8-2
ISBN-13: 978-0-9844142-8-4

SOLID OBJECTS
P. O. Box 296
New York, NY 10113

For you—

—at last.

Demonst(e)ration

"By its impossible form, the monster bridges the gap between contraries in aesthetic defiance of the logical rule: it provides the third term, the copula, the mediation, between all those entities doomed, by logic and language, never to be joined." (David Williams, *Deformed Discourse*)

In the laboratory secretly in the night stop there. In the laboratory out of the fragments of the dead and again halt. Entry in a journal, rem(a)inder, intimate: "July 24 [1816]: Write my story." *My* story: a slippage there. *Frankenstein*. To de-monstrate[1]: in the dead of night, alone in "my workshop of filthy creation" (a "cell, at the top of the house, . . . separated from all the other apartments")— living in my head—*now* I remember. One of the resurrection men[2] bangs a rusted shovel on the shut door, leaving a long streak of wet red clay. "Comparison and analysis need only the cadavers on the table; but interpretation is always producing parts of the body from its pockets, and fixing them in place." Origin one issue where—a "*collective* and *artificial* creature" which "cannot avail itself of the immense benefit of *totality*"—the body (of work) (and worker) dis-integrates at the site of an alienated labor: "my heart often sickened at the work of my hands." "*Quel siecle a mains!*" "[D]isturbed," "the . . . secrets of the human frame"

1 "De-monstration . . . transforms, it transforms itself, in its process rather than advancing a signifiable object of discourse" (Derrida: *La Carte Postale*).
2 A term for the 19th-century body-snatchers—who stole from graves (or otherwise produced) bodies to sell for dissection and study by medical students.

disturb a spectator: systems of articulation, of circulation ("…yellow skin scarcely covered the work of muscles and arteries beneath"), "which should have remained hidden," revealed, expose us. *Monstrum*, the word widening the world: "*She is neither one nor two … She resists all adequate definition. Further, she has no 'proper' name …*" Lost for a long moment beside the muddy puddle where you saw yourself for the first time and through borrowed eyes your own tears wept—wet to wet—long and always late by the dead author's lifted *montre*, warning that time decays beauties into "monstrous beings," while memory makes us each our own guest / (g)host. Acting out a strategy of identity on the unstable *Mer de Glace* language makes: "Ourself behind ourself, concealed / Should startle most— …" But "series of … being" as series of erasures or *seriasure*, this particular "dreadful collection of memoranda" functions to engender forgetfulness ("… a recipe not for memory but reminder"): this monster is re-membered in order to be dissolved in the same "darkness and distance" which swallows the text. Where we are recollected as, closing the book, "Not that": secured against otherness though "Decaying matter is so horrible a poison that certainly no aspects of the individual can provide protection." So much *about* the monster; what of the monstrous text? ("That I may reduce the monster to / Myself, and then may be myself …") Scraps of flesh sutured awkwardly down around disparate purchases and thefts: a 'crazy' quilt of mis-matched passages each (re)marked as the trace of a trace. Departing for parts unknown our fears are given deliciously terrible faces in the empty space at the curling edges of old maps, and though it turns out those ornate apparitions may have been drawn in part to protect the trade routes, one suspects a real horror of what resists definition also left its mark. But "how … [to] … speak 'otherwise,' unless, perhaps, we can *make audible* that which agitates within us, suffers silently in the *holes of discourse*, in the unsaid, or in the non-sense." On the long silver table, gleaming faintly along their damp borders in the intermittent light, the pieces that don't belong together; what's under discussion here in part(s) is syntax. In its desire for a mate the monster "raises the frightening possibility of a new and uncontrollable signifying chain, one with unknown rules and grammar …" Composition as de-composition: a series of positions where "A nice old chain is widening, it is absent, it is laid by." For life. The staggering progress of one for whom articulation is visibly thought. I remember her here who sat for her semblance: the portrait consisting "of multiple fragments … assembled under a new law"—*"But it doesn't look like me!"* *"Don't worry, it will."* "This shows the disorder, it does, it shows more likeness than anything else, it shows the single mind that directs an apple." We re(as)semble ourselves alone and out on the margins. "So the shape is there and the color and the outline and the miserable centre." Lurching toward you now with hands outstretched: to destroy? to embrace? "And I wished to exchange the ghastly image of my fancy for the realities around," the author of *Frankenstein* remembers, and the author of *Tender Buttons* remonstrates:

Supposing there are bones. There are bones. When there are bones there is no supposing there are bones. There are bones and there is that consuming. The kindly way to feel separating is to have a space between. This shows a likeness.

The *Monster* of us all, as in what once started can't be stopped: confessing the self to be a collage repeated interventions momentarily normalize as narrative. In the "I"'s an incommensurable loneliness. Essayed. To *Picture Show*: "So come up to the lab / And see what's on the slab ..." Frankly, Stein:

> *And how do you like what you are*
> *And how are you what you are*
> *And has this to do with the human mind.*
> "Identity a Poem"

Grave CITES

Beckett, Samuel. *Proust*. New York: Grove, 1931.

Benjamin, Walter. Translated by Harry Zohn. "The Work of Art in the Age of Mechanical Reproduction." *Illuminations*. New York: Schocken Books, 1969.

Brooks, Peter. "Godlike Science / Unhallowed Arts." *The Endurance of Frankenstein*. Berkeley: University of California Press, 1979.

Derrida, Jacques. Translated by Alan Bass. *A Derrida Reader*. New York: Columbia University Press, 1991.

———. *La Carte Postale*. Flammarion: Paris, 1980.

Dickinson, Emily. *The Complete Poems*. Boston: Little, Brown and Co.

Eliot, T. S. *Selected Prose*. New York: Harcourt Brace Jovanovich, 1975.

Freud, Sigmund. Translated by David McClintock. "The Uncanny." *Creativity and the Unconscious*. New York: Harper and Row, 1958.

Gauthier, Xavière. "Is There Such a Thing As Women's Writing?" *New French Feminisms*. New York: Schocken Books, 1981.

Irigaray, Luce. Translated by Carolyn Burke and Catherine Porter. *This Sex Which Is Not One*. New York: Cornell University Press, 1985.

Kristeva, Julia. Translated by Leon S. Roudiez. *Powers of Horror*. New York: Columbia University Press, 1982.

Moretti, Franco. *Signs Taken for Wonders*. London: Verso, 1983.

O'Brien, Richard and Sharman, Jim. *The Rocky Horror Picture Show*. 20th Century-Fox (England), 1975.

Plato. Translated by Benjamin Jowett. *Phaedrus*. Indianapolis: Hackett, 1995.

Poe, Edgar Allan. "The Short Story." *The Portable Poe*. New York: Viking, 1945.

Rimbaud, Arthur. Translated by Louise Varese. *Une Saison en Enfer & Le Bateau Ivre*. New York: New Directions, 1945.

Shelley, Mary. *Frankenstein*. New York: St Martin's Press, Bedford Books, 1992.

Slaughter, Frank G. *Immortal Magyar / Semmelweis, the conqueror of childbed fever*. New York: Collier Books, 1961.

Stein, Gertrude. *A Stein Reader*. Evanston: Northwestern University Press, 1993.

———. *Tender Buttons*. Los Angeles: Sun & Moon Classics.

Stevens, Wallace. *The Palm at the End of the Mind*. New York: Vintage, 1972.

Williams, David. *Deformed Discourse*. Montreal: McGill-Queen's University Press, 1996.

Installments:

(Etiology) Dreaming

Perspectives (Changing)
Cold. Couldn't move, couldn't control the size of things. "I."
My size. The city rubble from that height: the site of some
finished disaster. "Like." Or else it was green and damp and
warm on the underside of a leaf, though I shivered in the sud-
den wind and shadow your least movement made. Do you still
love me? My sighs. *I have a crush on you. Don't crush me.* The
song I meant "the sound" of metal crumpling in on itself, glass
splashing down on asphalt, the "deep audible respiration that
is usually a sign of grief": distant flames. Static in the long-dis-
tance connection. Voices faint. The words so loud in my head
I couldn't hear anything. Above it all a blurry star, a face. In the
night I believed would hide me. My signs.

Explanation (Easy)
"Fear of Intimacy." (As though we knew what that meant.) I
let someone close. I let him inside me. Only for a moment or
two. *Thank you. I'm sorry.* The smoke blew back on the salt
wind and I carried over the threshold a white heap of crumpled
sheets and dumped them in the machine as though to wash
away memory. Added bleach (on either side of the water): the
setting "hot" and "normal": end of that story?

Further Notes ("They Were Sleeping")
They were sleeping (an over-sleep) (already written out thor-
oughly). Played out. In a confusion of pronouns. ("Shadows of
the world appear . . .") The blackened rubble in which *We write
our reading*.

1

As in a Car Crash

I thought I could do nothing. I waited afraid to survive. I drifted through the echoing hallways saying only, "I wish you well," like the blank in the tale. Princess cesspool. Under a spell for a time, yes? The broken imagination repeating its one phrase, "He touched me …," beginning and ending. We held hands in the back of a patrol car watching the radar clocking abrupt changes of speed on a road where there was no one passing, nothing: maybe wind. Then I haunted all the places—like Café "Brainwash"—I hoped you might be.

Some Translucent Veils

Were in the way. Voices muffled. Faces blurry. (You. He.) Wisps of smoke rising and drifting gently away. "Like." "Like." After the door slammed I got up quickly, tore the sheets away …

Cold is a Typo

From down here the sole of your shoe is bigger than any house I could ever imagine building. From up there your movements— as you scurry or slither or file in formation back to your … — laughable, tiny. *Ha ha ha.* What was it you were going to give me?

Nothing / Car Crash

"You looked like a long term thing, and I'm not into long term things. Not right now at least."

Nothing / Car Crash

We both could've died. Cold have. Were going to die anyway. Hard to care, sometimes? You described the condition known as "Learned Helplessness" to me. Then decades of silence in a room strewn with those translucent, wilted, latex blossoms. Drafts. The candle guttered again, a little smoke trailed away. Weirdly awkward use of the second person. Saying nothing.

Explanations / Easy (For You To Say) (Therapy?)
He was afraid of me. We were both afraid: we were frightened, distrustful, attracted, sad already and (because it was over already) angry. *Sorrysorrysorry. And thank you* (for nothing). As in a nightmare, no movement, no sound, despite the gesture of running away, despite the screaming. Unless a whisper maybe. Who's listening? The sheets smelling as much of rubber afterward as anything. Words cut into the black night rolling over me. *"I saw stars."* Flattened a pattern I could read. I could tell you without looking. *Could*, I meant to write. Then, accidentally …

Autobiography
At once completely meaningless and more necessary to me than my own life, I thought that if he turned away—to someone else—I would die. If he left me. In a green shade. "I wish you well," was all I could say, figuratively stumbling over the long skirt of my invisible gown as I tried to drift past gracefully. From shining to shining. I had my work, didn't I? *Cut out for me.*

Symptoms
Without the courage to be hungry.

"Autobiography"
I kept looking down at the empty space beside me, as though there was a book there. In which I could read. Myself, my own heart. How to behave. I was so sick of being told how to behave:

I knew I was supposed to drift past gracefully. The gentle rustle of my garments the attraction of my vaunted inaccessibility. My name, my etymology. Father, I am reading; Father, I am bleached. The cycle paused, a rush of water in or out, and then continuing.

Some Translucent Veils
Turning and turning away.

Point of View
Where the web flew wide. I said "Don't hurt me," and he said, "But that's what I'm best at, it seems …"

Origin of the Species
The empty bed, the liberal traces of our impotence. Thinking.

From What Vantage (One of the States)
Inside a towering structure I had some small control over (as it moved through the world crushing whatever stood in its path) I cowered, miniscule in a dark crevice in what was known as the interior, humming what little I remembered of my various anthems, off key, clutching at my rags and hoping at once to be recognized and not to be seem, I meant to write "seen." I meant to write to the rest of the world (the world at rest) what I was, an apology, clumsy. Unfortunately my appalling pride got in the way. *Sorrysorrysorry.* My ride. Fuck you. Fuck me. "I wish you well." I watched the destruction happening far far far away, in another language, on a tiny screen. *Thank you again. Sorry.*

Symptoms
Alive, sort of, in the delay.

Perspectives Changing

She got up from her work. She put the mirror away and went to the window. Then she died. End of the story. You drive past unseeing, the light glitters back from shining chrome and the tower throbs slightly to the bass rhythms of whatever pop song it is you're blasting.

Sleep Explained

(Easy.) Close your eyes. She put the jagged pieces of the world away. To get me into bed you'd have said *anything*.

Dreaming

What it meant if you wanted to touch me. Me. You. Meaning. A green shade. Emergency. I would exist, finally. Oh, and you too. Naturally. What it meant if you called me, if you called me and I came. If you stayed hard long enough to penetrate ... My dream. And yours, carried over from when? What it meant if I let you touch me, if I let you touch me as just another better or worse one among the many. Already a memory. Whose sleep is this anyway? Hands off the wheel as we skidded—together whether we liked it or not—into the ditch of the next (century). Eyes closed. Mouths open as though we wanted to scream. Dreaming I'm sick of this. Screaming. The crumpled metal body and the broken glass. The crash as I drifted out gracefully.

In the Mirror

She thought the horse was a part of him: both of them covered in the same glitter, where the sun dazzled and flamed. A machine thought in a machine state. Statement made. Seamed. She thought he was part of the gun-metal blue twilight in which he, one of the moving pieces, gleamed. Maybe a misplaced part of the river's reflected shine. Dreamed. Impervious to pain. Because it was dangerous to admit to being vulnerable: as if it was the recognition that would finally end things.

Sleep Explained (Love & Kisses)

Go back to any previous section and test yourself to see how much of what you've read you've retained. Am I you, are you me? Say the words blacken under your gaze, the smoldering pages sift between your fingers as ashes when you try to look through them, or leaf … If you look away for a moment the meanings sear and escape. That book never existed. Trust me. Now the table is burning. Now I am burning, further, the words you remember, and you think that if you lie still enough, eyes shut, you will be allowed to re-enter that dream. *Cracked from side to side.*

Xxx

How laughable you are, my death, my love, how massive and how tiny: what a complete failure what an astonishing success. You're right not to answer my letters: it's true there's nothing either of us can say. And yet these gestures from the tower though you can't see or hear me, from the tower in which I am allowed to burn, to blow some kisses, to watch the mirror, to say, The car came to rest in a ditch and we stumbled back up to the road and you flung the not quite empty bottle of scotch into the slough just before the cops arrived. Yes I'm still, in answer to your question, a surrealist. A romantic. Waving. If you look up from the vanished page.

English / History

A little as heard. As half-heard. Identical positions guessed at (an "educated" guess)—or clear in the illustrated cut. But impossible to act out: not being divided (exactly) like that. Nevertheless. To start? "The brothers set out." *In the story.* The brothers set out, each (exemplary) instance "in search of the truth."

In the thin wall a fragile door painted to resemble a door swings shut: there. Now we're facing out. "Is this the pen? the box? the window? &c." Half-hearted? Nope, only just (*now*) learning to articulate.

The indefinite. Jangle of the hefted bridle echoing in the almost-empty stable he walks alone the length of, our example, our representative, our last hope … "In search of the truth"—or a truth … he could trust.

Guessing where the tongue should be? As shown. Facing now a foreign landscape familiar from dreams or fairy tales. Distance measured by the gestures made to travel through or abolish … To speak the language (I do / do not speak the language) or to make the correct sounds in the correct (*This your so beautiful, rich …*) … Spaces cut by breath. Once upon a time. "I do not speak the language." The lips are parted but only just. S-s-siblings. Setting out, each in turn, on a (re)quest.

A picture produced in the brain: the temptation to see it like that. A "picture" which, but this is absurd, would need yet another eye to see it and yet another after that to see the one who sees &c.; "What is the color of this box?"

After a period of waiting for his eldest brother to return, the next sets off. And so forth. In other words, not all at once. In other words, after a period of waiting (first leaves, then snow, then drops of rain slip past—they each adhere an instant and then fall in a smear as seen through the cracked … glass). First the first &c.: until only—his footsteps muted on the moldering hay but the bridle he brings jangling faintly in the huge, almost deserted stable—the youngest is left. Hope, then less hope, and then still less … headed toward the admission that hope was always false? A sort of stillness melting into the beginning of despair, and inevitably anger, then the need for some sort of action. *Saddle my horse!*

Aspirate Whisper Glottal Catch
(And the lips 'rounded')

Once upon a time—saddled with that from the start. In the illustrated cut the throat and mouth full of the symbols describing the action or rather the positioning of the tongue, at that instant. Bright leaves then snow then clumsy drops of water the same size as each traced "leaf" and "snowflake"; invisible wind the whole time, blowing against: curved lines to stand for the gusts? Road off into the subset. As seen: a jagged passage refracted in crazed or starred glass … as watched through the bright array of lines radiating from the hole where once …

"What color is the wall? Is the wall white &c."

Patterns of energy.
Let me remind you.

My brothers I resemble he says I am exactly like. Swings gently shut the thin door lest the wall painted to look like a wall come down upon it

Patterns of activity the object or all we know of the. Let me remind you, mutters an outgrown instructor, discussing again a lesson that couldn't be given to anyone else. I do not (part of the mouth contracted) speak fluently this, your so beautiful rich tongue … in this (you're so beautiful) country where we were, yes, to be assisted by hearing the words broken down into their essential elements, self-interpreting …

Did we believe that? The relief may have been in not having to believe it.

Exactly alike he asserts no way to tell us apart no really, as were our steeds, various shades of gray either fading out or increasingly dark so that the last—stamping in its stall at the end awaiting what I am told is my decision, my choice—is either A) White or B) Black. Or, see, fails to exist (except as promise).

A little as hoard. Distance measured by more or less significant changes in the wording of certain passages in the textbooks. Of the princess' previous suitors an example is made. "To tell the truth."

A flutter of the breath.
A quiver of the voice.

The heads of whose previous sexual partners—among them my brothers—are displayed here: a kind of demonstration. They failed, yes? *I'm a Stranger Here Myself.* You will please note that each, in a witty turn which makes them resemble nothing so much as a row of newly minted coins, faces the back of the head of the next, mouths open as if to address, as if halted mid-injunction, to halt. Or, Oh, excuse me, from behind you looked *just* like … The blood dries very slowly, you say it is a hereditary weakness? Is it true they cut their own throats? "They didn't take care of themselves"—this with a wave (toward the stinking barbaric display or to just to brush another one of those huge glittering flies off)—all this on the audio tour in which we are reminded our days are numbered. Each name to correspond to a stop, this amusing pastiche of fact, watered-down analysis, gossip, and contemporary mood music meant to make us feel pleasantly educated or just to keep us from speaking to each other any mild ideas—inspired by the exhibit—about a possible revolt. Each of them, after all, had had his turn as head of this our so beautifully ordered state. "Are these your books? They are our books." *Baise Papa, baise …*

The wall shuddering slightly when the door is shut no matter how gently so that the illusion … wavers for a moment

"Who is this lady? It is Mrs. West. Whose book is this? Whose coat is black &c." In the margin a neat little check

He finds himself in a clearing. He comes to. Again after every departure no letters and in the absence of letters always this imagination of the worst. *But as long as we can say it is the worst* … Dark as (k)night or completely colorless, your choice. Believe me your servant (yours, earnestly &c). ("The symbols appear at some disadvantage, from the comparative coarseness of the experimental types, and in the absence …"—such is the so-called *clearing*: the site where all recalled communications break off.)

Walking the length of that crumbling stable with him, "ears pricked," or even, so we imagine, *as* him, ears packed with the recorded jangle of a lifted bridle and a description of the almost smoky scent of moldering hay along with the mild sweet stink of drying horse shit. Whore's shit. *This must've been a stable once* &c. (If you'll look to your right …). In one hand the bridle, *ching*, in the other, extended, an apple; fingers well away from the fruit, palm kept carefully flat. End of side A.

Glass starred in the little window of the door shut precipitate

From the other side the heads are seen as halved. To see the works or how they work, or *if*. Airily, "Not now, of course!" He sits in the middle of the road this is somewhat later looking through his saddlebags hoping to find the manual exactly halfway on his or the way to the rescue or what he can still in the absence of letters imagine is "the rescue." Our home life? Driven from the lungs the breath ascends, encountering a (shifting) resistance. My only sons. (In whom I am well squeezed.)

(To tell the truth.)

From the other side as pressed against the glass: The Organs of Speech. Each human head iterative in cross-section but for the slightly differing positions of. As if they each took up the same tale but in a slightly different place? To illustrate. (But what? I'd guess it's up to us—we are her subjects after all—to guess?) (I cannot pass the test—and so I pass it: like that.)

"Son et Lumiere" promised every night and every night put off again until the next. The excuse the threat of "precipitation" but the signs misleading or not read aright. The anticipated system shifts off the map—if in fact it exists. In memory the tower on the bridge remains the illuminated enclosure of unseen characters, pure voice-over, still able to *encore* the juicy bits. Of love and politics, of love, which is and is not politics. Rough hum of generators. The very stones their secrets &c. Clouds of insects in the floodlights this loosed chaos of musical notes.

In the middle of the journey? "In a fix." I am, how do you say, a poor mechanic. *Break it anew*, the extent of the advice. Maybe it's past time to admit that each one was in fact a substitute; "Poor," he murmurs, picking up and setting down again what doesn't work, each lifted part he can't make fit &c., "substitute." Sour apes recite again, The princess is an old bitch (frustrate) gone in the teeth? Check the textbooks: it isn't only your brothers she took, she takes. *How Long Has This Been Going On*, the tune tinkling out over the black water and the unsteady reflection of the dramatically lit historical site—a tower pieced together from assorted chunks of broken monuments.

He dries his mother's tears or tries to and then sets, as set down in the story, off. Each one in turn. And if he is her last hope he must also be or so he believes the final hope of yet another woman also seen as weeping 'in the mind's eye,' her younger face far less distorted by the act. At the highest window of a distant tower &c. Watching the road in the mirror. He takes the route his brothers took and also turns to wave at the fork where they before him also turned to wave one last … A collection of numskulls, she mutters, putting by the crumpled, graying bit of white lace she holds to her eyes only at moments like this, adding that it was from this exact same window (point of view) she'd watched the departure of her ex. (Which?)

"The black book is <u>on</u> the table. The red book is <u>under</u> the table. The table is <u>before me</u>. The wall is <u>behind you</u>. <u>I am</u> in front of the window." Believe me &c. your servant, a poor relation writes.

The bridge the eye recognizes as a section of the tower, or the tower itself say floating horizontally as seen in a series of mirrors and lenses worn on a kind of harness for around three days to correct for the inversion. Why translate? A reduplicated, not a missing part, no use trying to make it fit where no absence—as yet—allows it a permanent address. Unable to locate the blind spot. "The harmony is found to consist in having our experience meet our expectations." Susceptible of a multitude of modifications affecting the pitch. This box. A beautiful, rich &c … lived in a country far far away under a curse &c. Their streets paved with gold and so forth. Seen in the cracked glass disjunct or diffracted as though sections of time had been edited out.

He refuses in these parts to recognize himself.

Pierced by high narrow windows the tower, within another larger tower, within another yet. In a fix; as re-presented. The guards imagine chucking the tombstones (out of which the edifice was constructed) one by one into the stillest of pools (nothing ever happens on these long, these seemingly endless shifts); meanwhile those guarding *them* experience an unslakable thirst: the recorded sound of lightless water always in their ears. (Nevertheless.)

"Saddle my horse!" But the grooms are long gone, the family fortune lost in outfitting expedition after expedition, none of which ever came back. A series of inventions he says explaining his lack of progress which however or so he insists might in time point out *an* unexplored way if not *the* way toward *a* if not *the* truth. Of course there was a deadline for her rescue, which, although always extended, each one managed to miss. Nonetheless. An airy wave toward the mounting evidence: *Hearts and minds*—"They didn't believe in themselves!" His brothers are *history*, a passage in the textbooks, those sections dealing with this period given more or less space in subsequent runs as previous editions are replaced. The gist of it a gesture on the part of some sub-sub-editor with sometimes a political ax to grind but most often just a job at stake. Just? Did I say *just*? The past. Cold and numbered now among the august Heads of state. O gust. It's difficult. It's harder than it looks. The vibrating edges (only) produce the sound called voice.

"Mr. White, take this book. What does Mr. White do? He takes the book. Open the book. What does Mr. White do? He opens the book. I open the door. What do I do? (You open the door.) Please, close the door." The gate is shut the lights are off the bridge is raised the tower is only a memory; the night is … —I am speaking here your language dark (as night), my mouth cut open to the throat. These words. Pleas: clothe the whore.

Thought of what they encountered as a series of necessary tests but of course it was only the preface—the echoing voice of her absent father tendering his dearest possession & so forth: I sieve you this sand and barrage. Nevertheless. Too many times dubbed in and over that mumbling seems still to be originating on the site where a doubled lookout once defined the skyline for us. Get on with it then, his mother sighs, blowing out her lips like a horse.

He confuses her garments with her flesh.

The bridge belongs, he reads, to neither side of the abyss. (But the work of crossing it …)

In their cold ears always that voice which seems to arrive from the direction of the river. *Drink To Me Only With Thine Eyes*. The riven. The lover (in a line[up] of lovers). These rivals. Apply ever after.

Their purpose always presented as Coming To the Rescue or that was the speech they stumbled through at the prodding of the officials, the same stilted phrases, each archaic excuse. I had thought that here, at last, &c. Has anyone you don't know asked you to carry something for them? An uncertain shake of the head. Eyes shifty, yes? I admire your traditions. The contents of the saddlebags strewn on the greensward; a couple of lap dogs yapping in the midst of the mess. What is the nature of your business? Each one, or so it's said, found the implicated towers completely empty though closely guarded by a man of glass. From the room above (access barred) a blur of voices assigning flight paths. What happened to that central truth? Your gust is as good as mine. No, please, you must be *my* ghost.

Rode often off into the upset, unable to speak of the sun's last light, lush pinks and an orange-y rose, a coral color? Day's stain as seen through a haze of chemical dust, too—after all that's passed— … "romantic." Nevertheless.

A voice close to if not in fact that of his mother reminds him that her eldest (and so then each of them) "merely" followed in his father's footsteps. If he could go back now he'd try to get what he sees *in his mind's eye* actually painted on the cracked path he remembers in front of the house—not far from Echo Park—instructions as for some complex dance step: the black and white positions, numbered, of the gendered feet. Left. *Right.* Left

"One sound … haunted the ear and the mouth by day and night, 'seeking rest but finding none;' and with it flitted a train of obviously kindred sounds, clamoring for recognition." Supply fevered laughter.

Each steed a lighter shade until the last, blind, fat as a maggot—perfectly colorless. Each steed a darker shade until the vast stable's only remaining inhabitant, starved in the farthest box, 'dark as night,' 'coal black' &c. is led into the light for the last son's look, and bitter laugh: "A knacker's hack, but," laying a heavy hand on the trembling flank before they take it back, "it ought to do the trick."

An illegible scrawl in the thick dust on the cracked mirror glows in the fading light

"Do I open my book? Close your book. Do you close your book? Does Mr. White close his book? Take this pen. Who takes this pen?" In wholly patrimony. To each one she says the same last words: "You look like someone I loved once." The final tower neither exists nor does not exist. How is that?

A discarded horseshoe, a rusted nail, a bit of frayed rope seem— scattered on the ground in the clearing where he's set up this improvised encampment, this service station of the mind, the re- pair site he's repaired to until the repairs are finished—to come to say he isn't the first to be offered this possible out, the collapse of his useless mount: a last 'last chance' to actually tell a story— about ...? Knowing his brothers as well as, he says, himself, he knows how each would have gone on somehow, hurrying to, as it turned out, replicate the exact fate of the one before him, prefer- ring a stuttered catastrophe perceived as personal, more purely willed, to what could have been dismissed as an accident. He picks up a foreleg, puts it down, and again picks it up. He draws a horse in the dirt, extra lines for the several positions of its legs as he imagines they might—at isolate moments in time—appear in movement. He should've been studying veterinary tracts, not the troubadour poets. He crouches under the lifted leg trying to see what the matter is, which is to say trying to see how it would go if there weren't anything the matter: a state of affairs it isn't, any longer, possible to imagine much less access. "But you can't say I don't have a hoof over my head at least." Heh heh. Laughs at his own jokes: lies down amid discarded packaging on a bed of dust.

Did you love your brother?
Which?

At the first of the many the infinite so it's said forks in the road (it's nothing but forks, that road, crux after crux) each one paused—deceptively or so it seems, as if still deciding, at that late date—and waved once. Stalled there and then repeated the exact … When in fact the bravest gesture, the impossible gesture, his mother remarks, would have been to turn back. Back turn to, he teases her, as they watch the penultimate set off with that same little hitch and final blind wave, been would gesture impossible gesture bravest fact in when. God, oh, she says, returning to her loom, Up shut.

"I go out of this room. Who is going out of this room? Where do I come from? Does Mr. White go out of the room? No sir, he remains in it." Layers of graffiti deface the narrow pass as if to testify that at just this juncture each of the previous travelers was also treated to the illusion—if that's what it is—of the home they'd just departed from going up in greasy smoke.

Each one as he arrived displaced another discovered in possession and unrecognizable in that: in other words, each one insisted on rescuing her again, from the previous success. Was it success? In as much of her story as we ever get it seems she's equally happy or unhappy enough with all of them. *How do you measure*, she asked or the structure itself seems to ask in the reenactment, *happiness?* No one can explain why they never got around to writing the letter that would have said "Arrived safely," &c. We were so busy at that point, and then, it seemed, almost at once ... Each brother upon his arrival finds a closet full of barely worn outfits at first a little too large and later a little too tight. No time for funerals or any sort of fuss: their bodies donated, each in turn, to science—for the further glory of the State.

Did you love your brother?
As myself.

Our home life: a hypothesis tested against another hypothesis. They are our books. They are our hosts. Pronounciated. Please: be/leave me your servant

Each one, having waved once a little at random as to watchers unseen and not quite fully believed-in, halts for a moment as if choosing which of the ways to take though evidently it's only a matter of more or less time as both roads, by all accounts, wind up in pretty much the same place.

Every love, or so I've heard (and do in part believe it), most real in the instant of replacement, evoked as lost. In tears, she tells you what she told the judge, In the end ... in the end I really couldn't tell them apart. Each lover, having heard her in silence, walks—when she leaves them alone in that room—to the cracked glass to study their face for the resemblance.

The bridge collapses. The tower plunges, as they say, into the abyss. In the open passage no sound. Inside the tower another tower, yes? And each prince takes up the work of restoration— studying the plans deep into the night—where the last left off. Each one confessing, in the words another used, that he is no architect, but

"Resting," he's passed by two riders, one on a white horse, one borne by a black. Both are richly caparisoned: feathers and jewels—as they race off in opposite directions—nod and flash. One messenger flourishes a gold-trimmed scroll, one holds out a black-bordered envelope, each leans into the lather-flocked neck of a laboring steed shouting instructions or encourage- ment now—in the pounding of hooves and the jingle of metal and creaking of leather—lost. He tries to memorize the motion: he rocks a bloody jawbone across his knee or goes looking for what's left of the legs, coughing a little in the raised dust, the road still slightly throbbing, or so it seems, with that diminish- ing beat.

Each lover crosses the threshold with the same phrase on his lips: "She belongs to *me*."

Each time the same degree of exactly the same resentment: flash of the lifted blade and a warm wet red silky curtain flow- ing across the cracked mirror where each meets the reproachful eyes of . . . his mother?! A dulling gaze searching the murderer's face. His own face. Take this. *Sand in marred age*. A perfect match.

In fairy tale or in some version of fact, wolves—slavering a bloody froth—would by now have carried both disassembled steed and discouraged suitor off. As if to say But there is no word in your language for ... or I am not speaking perfectly this, your so beautiful, rich ...

Behind him, or so he imagines, she remarries—left at last to her own devices—no one left to attempt to dissuade and finally wave off. "Bring forth men-children only," her latest husband murmurs, returning from the wars to find her worked up about a letter he sent, in the middle of a conversation about something else.

The patterns of activity the parts arrive as in the brain are not enough to animate what's left (in disarray) of what he hoped would get him to the end of this. He could pick up the saddle and walk of course, but the thought of arriving like that—as if he were simply a section of the road itself ... articulated ... completely covered in dirt ... "What do you want," or, worse, the "Can I help you," said—not asked—in that tone which means *get out*. My brothers are dead and I am alive, he repeats the suggested phrase, then, adds, despite himself, "but." My brothers are dead but I am alive. There is a silence, tape hiss, and then his voice goes on, the tone curiously flat: But unlike me they did not feel their lives were meaningless.

Ahead of him, or so he remembers from his reading, she remarries—not ever given time enough to get to what she calls her own work, to find her *voice*. The suitors arrive like waves, like waves, breaking across a smooth stretch of sand: each one completely annihilates the last. If she sings in this racket, she sighs, it's precisely so as not to have to hear herself. Hopeless, she says—with a laugh.

Haunted by the luminescent dream of the quick fix: We'll have you on your way again in no time! As though it never happened. Drive or derive-thru everything or else the fetishization of some idea of craftsmanship: the recuperation of every difficulty and heart-deadening set-back as "a time of growing and changing." Amid the carnage … In a deserted clearing … "Are you sorry not to be an American?" A practice question. Days pass. An interview with the remains of the means of passage, a rider halted mid-career in converse with what, literally, came apart (in progress): "I just wanted to get somewhere." Awake in the middle of the night to hear the hoof beats diminish, to hear the hoof beats draw near and again diminish, he halves the head of the horse, writes its history, offers to teach it what he laughingly calls his language, Anguish ("'A' is for apple," holding the fruit just out of reach), nourishes his dreams of a shared, perfect alphabet; he gives his guest a past: stable in the stable expecting (with and without reason) the same thing every day. I am explaining you slowly this. His dreams? "Increasing loneliness."

At last she admits that she's never been married: "Sure, I've dated a lot of guys, but …"

In a deserted clearing to stop and think of what … —halted, forced into thought—stuck. Or to set up a roadside stand

and sell what's left and not yet (if you don't come too close or breathe, much) *totally* spoiled, under the name of another kind of meat? To stop on the way to the glue factory and see what more you can get for the odd bits; to sit and wait there, one bloody thumb poised to tip a little extra onto the already heavy price? "It all adds up." To sit there yourself like yet another juicy slice (of life)? Or to disrupt the economy—if you can— even if only by refusing to participate: to take the thing apart looking for that finality of form they said you'd recognize when you saw it, looking (in other words) for a way out?

A little as *whored*—against R-ruin. "What is the organ of thought? Where is the brain situated? Do you think of your lessons when you are not here? What did you think of at your last lesson? Can you speak correctly without thinking?"

Each brother—after the first sets off and fails either to reappear or send word of his safety or whereabouts—waits out a period exactly measured by the gradual erosion of hope into sorrow, the collapse of sorrow into anger, the spontaneous combustion, finally, of anger into the need for action, foretold by the inevitable boasts, and then the ostentatious polishing—to a mirror-like shine—of the already gleaming armor. And then? "Saddle my horse!" A sort of pep rally around the departing warrior less and less convincing as the number of players on the home team shrinks. "Throwing good money after bad," their mother mutters under her breath in the hoof-rattled courtyard of a castle always a little less loud with shouted encouragement, advice &c.

Their heads were halved, it is explained, to open a space for enquiry. Our home life?

Articulating the claim to ownership each one uses, she notices, not only exactly the same words and tone but in fact the voice of the other: as if spoken *through*. "Explain 'right' and 'wrong' by examples, as: *I think you are an American; am I right or wrong?*" Within the tower another tower &c., each one more tower-like, more the tower you think of at once when given the instructions: *Think of a tower*... A bunch of dummies. The heads were halved, it is reiterated, because that is what they're *really* like.

"Someone," she amends, "*I thought* I was in love with once."

"Are you writing anything? Yes I am writing my English exercises. What are you doing? Nothing." Our home life: compare and contrast. Opened to illustrate, an educational practice belonging to a pedagogy all but abandoned though no study had convinced us of its uselessness: opened in the illustrations along that "natural" line he was so fond of pointing out to us to show exactly where the tongue should be in the instant / between one sound and the next. "Yourself, myself, ourselves &c. should be well-practiced by questions like: Whom do you see in a looking glass? (yourself) Whom do I see in a looking glass? &c." Elaborate rituals around the precisely timed changing of the guard (the spectators meant to remark as they often do that *it's just like a dance*) ("It's just like a dance") enacted not to hide but to make more apparent the fact that at the end of the intricate exercise each returns to what seems to be exactly the same place.

And above our unhorsed hero—full-stopped mid-stride amid the remains—still trying to repair what he took apart long ago to evocative fragments or merely wandering from part to part in a state of wonder (how, if ever, did these edges go together?), does the moon come up, as the poet asks, as the moon? Which? A hoof in each hand, he clops the gory road he'll no more ride: a Foley artist of sorts, for the flick of a hope not in fact his own, yet by him—or so it seems now—lost. When this comes up for you, the analyst asks, what else comes up? Does the soundtrack *demand* tears: sack the art and score the rind? Does he solace himself with others' words? *Do you want to talk about it?* Clop, clop. The honeymoon each brother had was all too brief, interrupted as it was almost at once by yet another suitor. But one could also, so he tells himself, tell oneself that each, cut down in the flower of their passion (save the penultimate—awaiting, at the bloody hands of his bride's next bachelor, a constantly deferred reprieve from what they are both, by now, increasingly sour, describing as "the relationship"), lived a honeymoon which lasted *forever*. Clip-pity clop. Meanwhile his own failure to arrive, anywhere. A glimpse of peace among the pieces of the vehicle, his cry a weak counter-tenor: *Hang up the phone?* Where was it you first felt the tooth? *Uh huh.*

"We see them during the night. In the sky. In the West

The heads are halved, or so it's said in the literature, to ensure there will be no going back over territory if not conquered then certainly covered. Recovered. History has made us certain promises. Hangs a sign there, Do Not Touch. The light angled and reflected from those ashen cheeks (history made us) hazed by the ash of the fallen structure into oranges and pinks, a flush as of health. We hold these dudes to be self-evident; held open as a book, to read there what we were promised we would also someday feel and think.

A bit of rope, the rusted and bent nail from a thrown shoe, a scrap of torn or burnt paper bordered in black, or tarnished gilt … There is evidence the others also, although the authorized sources are mute, might have found themselves in a similar tight spot: broke, taking the thing apart along the lines laid down for its consumption, being careful with the choice cuts, joint by joint, and then trying—once more but with a difference—to make it all add up. Cut into the furthest stronghold or so it's said a slot or slit through which the interactions of the whirling colored lines seem to intersect—in what is perceived as a *causal relationship* …

Nevertheless.

Our home life in the region of the waterfall, in expectation of the projected improvements, along the lines laid down by a road made up of alternate versions of that road, blossoming where the fractured rigidities of a choose-your-own-adventure story inevitably discover our hero as the assistant assistant manager of a struggling franchise, shucking half his grease-spattered livery to get it on in a restroom with one of the kitchen help, whose troubles with the native tongue prove no bar to communicating what's keeping the custom away: rumor is it's mostly, what they're selling, horse meat. Unrolling a condom, hooking her tiny thong of grayish lace down from behind, our hero lifts his subordinate's uniform and bends her over the basin, watching himself in the mirror. Employees must wash their hands before returning to work, she uncertainly sounds out. He bites her neck to keep her in place. "This action illustrated yields a *hushing* sound, *sh*." Speak to me only of your liquid assets

The heads we have are haven—or they half us? *What* picture? he asks irritably, dousing the light, setting the clock again for the expected arrival of his brother, an overdue visit, constantly put off. Those who've gone before are a series of classic busts: coins stuck in the slots on a cardboard foldout, a place to press a piece of change if you're feeling generous, to join the fight against … —whatever, to do your part. Warm oil already turning one corner of the bag translucent as you set out, well-provisioned. These late additions to what were we given (as shadows "fell") of the black or white figure of our lady of the two freedoms, the instructions-for-assembly themselves a work of art. A collection of half-truths, he says with a self-consciously airy wave, dismissing the transcription: It all depends on how you look at it.

"Yellow leaves then rain then snow then rain then flowers and green leaves"—as cut out of construction paper: a jagged orange shape, a faded blue stiff sack or drop arrested in its fall, a perforated, doily-like, precisely creased and slightly grimy bit of white stuff, and so on, each symbol held by a single thumb-tack high up amid the questions, lists of names, encouraging slogans, and test dates.

A rumor runs among collectors: some early editions have it that the brothers, each deposed in time, but still alive, fail to return because they're restless, addicted to the quest, just can't stay home, too anxious to go out again and rescue the next tall pale sad princess or lady-in-waiting and yet another after that &c. Or it's the lure of the significant funds invested in the Defense budget. "Saddle my horse!" Close the door behind you please the only thing she ever said for *their* ears, or so they claimed, the rest of her address saved for the mystery man she insisted each of them very nearly was but couldn't quite exactly recreate (in her heart). The inside story is the heads were halved to make it seem like there were more of them, who would have stayed but were by her or by her need for solitude themselves left. Doubled in the juggled books to bolster up her worth. *I vant to be alone*, she practiced. If you are not a native speaker the text will be closed, but the pictures themselves, it's said, 'tell a story' which should be clear enough.

A collection of half-wits.

Intended 'structural improvements' yet to be deciphered through a bleary cross-hatch of half-erased revisions, ragged flecks of India rubber black w/ lead and the smeared sweat of the dubious architect, beside himself, who says we shouldn't call him that. ("Don't call me that.") Yet each one sat down once with a satisfied sigh to the luckily unfinished task, happy to think he'd found a way to both respect the history of the project and to, gosh, well, blushing, make a name for himself. Glad to escape awhile the importunate cloying manipulations of that damsel still, for all his efforts, as much as ever in distress.

So much depends on whether or not the patterns are accepted as representing objects.

Our home life in the general area of the actual, near but not near enough. The fluster of covering endless discrepancies jarred our interactions into stiff cliché or clumsiness. Our mother in black, turning away well before whoever it was this time reached the final bend in the road, speaking of God's will, preferring "closure" at any price. *You can let go now.* At the instant of departure we can't help but make more or less inadvertently clear to our hosts our deep and abiding indifference. What we needed was only their brief esteem or "faith"? A roof. Were we just pretending to enjoy ourselves or is it that that belief is what matters most in this instant? "Once upon a time." Our home life a lame excuse for our home life. Interspliced with a dream of escaping, as seen on p. 1, in which we invented, in the highest, least visited room in the last observation post, a princess who badly needed help (the really excellent part beginning "Bravely"). A trope we ourselves believed by the epilogue, each night's segment of which ended in exactly the same image: eerily silent wolves tearing at and then consuming every trace of the-horse-you-rode-in-on while an unnerved rider works his wireless phone from a precarious branch &c.

"What am I doing? I move the table. Do I move my head? No, I hold it still. I am writing; do I move my hand? Yes sir, you do."

We know how the works worked once but not what to do now they don't. Hence this collection of memorized moments ... — impossible to think your thinking like that. As in fact it isn't dancing when you still wonder which ... which foot. Forward back. Buck up! The heads are halved they said as that's the only way the truth can get to us. *Which?* As you might get in this case a horse through the narrow eye of a beholder having broken its gallop down into a series of stills and thence to the component dust. Almost, at this point, frantic.

Denoting the "catch" of the breath heard (with percussive violence) in a cough

Lumiere & Sons as promised. Aspiration, these lines thrown back, through belief, into throats the revolution halved, lost loves left out too late tonight or simply unperformed in these unequal parts, implicating each expression of terror caught like that forever in a basket of sawdust. Hard kiss of the blade on each neck and each head set aloft later for better instruction as a series of photos of the moon in the same phase might punctuate (as ellipses) a black background meant to represent the night sky in another clime for us. Not *tonight*, of course, but

Or she said: "You look like someone." And, "I was in love with *'once'*." Half-hearted. Our home life of associations the ruptured sequence ...

Come here.
Go there.

A little as hard to hear, growing fainter. The language of my people. The language of my country. (Describe difference.) Here, in this (your so beautiful &c.). Sounds, how do you say, estranged? Did you understood? Face to face with the foreign word, we set the sons we thought in part we were a little while loose, "like wolves." The shadings are difficult. "Contracted to a narrow chink, the breath in passing sets the edges of the orifice—the 'vocal ligaments'—in vibration, and creates sonorous 'voice.' This vocalizing condition of the glottis is pictured in the Symbol."

The other thing they all said or had to say: "Take that!" And then came as we say to themselves, horrified, the instrument (in that instant falling from nerveless fingers) the same the dying victim once used himself … —&c. The exact same look of horrified recognition even then on his face. *Which?* The same fractured river light reflected dancing on the lifted blade and back from the broken glass.

"Do not come here: remain there. Are you coming here? This is my place, and that is your place. Are you at your place? Come here. Go to your place. What are you doing?"

Once upon a time. To tell the truth. A heat shimmer blurred this stonework trembling a thirst shuts

Completely unutterable
Nevertheless

Spectrograms
(projected autobiography)

I have no body; the "I" writing this has no body: not in the old way. Zones. Pressures. Here a structural tension there an underlying ache. Vital signs. Phases of disquiet not clearly demarcated from areas of peace. In the insurgency someone hauling out the old slide projector, everyone else preparing—*Here let me freshen that drink*—to more or less sleep. A test case—an intermediary attempt, closely monitored—they don't say that *just* to be reassuring. What's thought of as two distinct systems, existing in an uneasy but highly functional state of irritation. No active rejection on either side. As yet. "As yet" as pulse. The question of damage held open. Reassurance wired in to excite a mirroring response? A collection of preparations, earlier versions, later models, mistakes. *A Sentimental Journey*. No sudden movements. "See, it's a *sand* painting." The dream of being perfectly understood coagulating briefly into grainy legibility. Doses of light. The *two* systems (because they're easier to see like that), sitting down at the [televised] table, in dialogue *at last* as the analysts echo for an audience tuning in late—"This is us in … where was that, darling … Darling?" Next

Who's the "we" in "We were so civilized"? Another holiday. To across you articulate distance. Hydraulics of syntax, sections of greasy steel appearing out of nowhere suddenly. Mash notes as scribbled calculations in the margins of the blueprints. Structural condolences. Soldering so delicate you could miss the seam: "nobody." Two days in 'the shop' to refrag the memory. A flare or amplitude of *feeling* could freeze the whole thing, fixed in position awaiting the arrival of the paid attendants zoned-out on the drugs that make it possible to handle me. This is us at the airport, the train station, in a—what did they call them there?— … a kind of illness, a taxi. Hysterical mixture of flesh and. I'm a warning. With the proper meds and only after intensive training: a hand that's steady. In the slippages cited heartaches replace "me." Relieved to be left to my own devices, as they say. Frequencies. Only

Constant breakdowns built in still shocking. An early stage of the research, flesh "sensing" the machine as too cold, and the machine—reacting badly to its experience of the meat environment: read as oppressively "hot," even dangerously … Relocate. *Who wants another drink?* To call the system dual is to increase the territory of an error but I or we continue to describe everything in terms of unstable binaries-that-bleed. Intervening. Parts of parts, halfheartedly self-inventing, utilizing available material in combinations at once tired and totally unforeseen. Blank surface of denial warmed by distant explosions: that one's backward, just look at the writing. To exist in the discrepancies. Etched in the edgy confession to avoid … Expecting

Surface roughened. "Rubble" as if seen from a satellite. Resonant influences. Omitting the non-relevant features of the phase. Turn of prefabricated substitute in the flesh sheath. Casual kindness causing a more or less ragged check in the gliding hum of *I don't feel anything* under the mantra-like hiss *Accomplishment*. Even the lightest, most casual, rudeness might overwhelm tiny interlocking gears already under strain, frugal lubrications—doled out by the-system-that-knows-best—already sizzling off. Wisp of *What the* … Cordite tang. Then this fevered "thin skin" fries the finger a clumsy mechanic waves in the air, like a lit match: "Fuck!" Uninflected frames walked empty through the air: spaces for a question that doesn't get asked. Unprocessed regret, incomplete collections of details in some always inadequate assemblage: "We always meant to go back, but …" Shifting in the dimness. Already wetting down the blistered digit in his mouth so it comes out "Whuck!" Degrades at timed intervals to delay rejection of components. A prototype. Not, I repeat, a success. Not "yet." *Always room for improvement* the technicians say in passing, giving one side of the thing a whack with a spanner, for luck. Built to spec under constant

Description. Apparently arbitrary sequence of condensations and cloudy orbits, wind-animated expanse, granular beliefs launched in overlapping elliptical drift. Shadow-crossed drag of hesitant glottal stops veer off either side in an ether of scrimped estimates. "Well it looks like …" I'm the manual ('in the flesh') wherein to read is to dissect. Skimming back off the burn point. And out. Translate. To be frank they left the leaving mechanism inside to go after the always retreating detritus: *You knew what I meant*, etc. Another tourist trap. Stifled laughter stretched taut through these perforations. To sit again through the trip: bodiless but detailed to the point of

Somewhere a gap and for a few days it's down. Multiple intensities also numbness. Sizzle. "This is us at …" A certain stiffness in the seen comes to stand for how real it seemed, once. Before the crash a wheezed scramble of signals: each term infecting the other, unable to find what separates. Wait. Where sinew meets wiring what's nobody's fault or everyone's flinches once: "In the [rhymes with], where the sun never … [rhymes with]." Parts constantly being replaced so identification requires a complex and increasingly lengthy series of always less effective procedures. Amplitudes of dismayed shock and "hopelessness." Increasing fortifications of a reiterated fragility that already bores us finds its way through the forest alone: this afterimage of sparks still flaring between us. Watched them slamming lockers, clocking out. A collection of "residual ideologies." As if what didn't work more certainly exists or in its non- or malfunctioning draws an inflamed attention to itself and (retained in the next stage as irritated memory "tissue") stays frozen in that configuration—despite constant tinkering, assurances, and the apparent lack of further problems—to be remembered as broke. Loosen *that*

Fizz of fire-punctured air, then a cathedral of light—upside down—and a smiling sun-burnt couple apparently falling headfirst into emptiness. You're right there *is* something wrong. A limited set of possibilities viscous in the adherence to what can feel like presence. Waits for reappraisal, reactivation. One goal to "feel better" than this. Each operation involves a series of calculations taking both crisp untenanted future and soggy crowded past into account. Constant expansions and contractions factored in in cracks and panics. What works sounds like (laughter) and then I am also (trying to laugh). Using the recordings: some critical section falling to the oil-stained concrete floor with a defeated clank. *Time for a smoke break.* They lift the

thing out and look at it disgusted for a moment. Sheers past—
that shimmer—something (to) something (about)

Dull rainbows snarled in spilled grease, fuzzy loudspeakers
dispensing "motivations." Everything turning to technique.
Turning? Shakes down into a tin-can-clatter dragged off. Con-
gratulations trash. Everything a question of skill and cleverness
or luck, each interchangeable part infinitely replicated, marked
down, must go. *Likeness*: a chemical breeze rustling shreds of
lists. Whose vanished breath. That sunset again and again the
big oily wave that won't—held up for admiration—ever crash.
Burning off the residue of an interior an abruptly stifled laugh.
But I don't recognize it. Not

On "automatic" the system operates a blind series of counter-
tactics based on more or less reliable information "fed" through
flawed instruments. Anxiety shreds the taut "just getting
through" recursion. Hoarded bits of disparate recollection form
a functional model for future performance. "We were happy
once." Where they run the predetermined assessments again
until the results open further distances, intricate, and the noto-
riously nimble fingers embroider information's safe passage in
plastic. Under everything a blank disbelief and over everything
this always less convincing imitation. The trick is to keep

The image generating mechanism makes uneasy guesses at
what life might have been like given the information and after
awhile why not: "I" extends into these versions as not particu-
larly well-informed or deep, but gee, awfully nice. Again the
blurred impression of some sort of monument. I *am* just like

my father (in his white coat). Light off the upended edges of the socioeconomic. Sibilant hiss of escape. Totally panicked for a moment like I actually had a childhood outside that beaker of smoking, fizzing muck lifted up so the security camera could get a load of it. "Eureka!" Pssssst. "Voice activated, remote controlled, capable of an early response." The personal touch! Shipped in from off-shore where the deft touches of those slender brown fingers (used to more intricate handiwork still infused with religious significance though now mostly produced for the tourists whose fear of and interest in the other takes the form of an anxiety to purchase) brings this corporate fantasy to. Crisis. Pride bolted to a shriek of don't touch it don't move it don't. Reduced or expanded to their supportable version of fact. Then a chill florescence off the faintly rippled surface of the vats, and this facsimile of a hand they make me wear (so much less upsetting for observers) "like ice." Like

"I" meaning solitary explanation or wedged sideways where something won't shut a kind of stopgap. Isolated resemblance. Do you believe bits of what happened to you open under lights and anesthesia will come back? A write off. Kiss until. Insinuate. Tinkling O you were so cute! Before the. Next. Next

One of the technicians stumbles past, and (as though the switch was where it always was)—"That's me with …"—slaps the wall by the door once or twice. "Dark," with all its connotations, chars each retreating chance. Wounded in unacknowledged ways less by hopelessness than the necessity of pretending *not* to be hopeless, right next to "we the people," where the directions for assembly start. "Shivered the whole night through" at the barbed-wire gate where they were patted down and then x-rayed before being let out. What's "free" flares up each morning and blacks out again each night. The wives they keep the horrors of the working day from turn aside to seek out faster results. In segments they beg me to recognize and bless, it all comes back. Mobilize an organic "essence" remaindered from earlier versions. In that place it finally seemed necessary to assimilate only the capacity to imitate. Still the dazzling screen and unsynched soundtrack, grinding to a semi-halt. Out of which something further seeps? If it went well they were "proud" of me, if it went badly I didn't exist. This eye has no buddy, I practice as if

Rhythmic. Mangled strategies for containment complete themselves as echoed chorus. In the intervals permitted adjustments: connections less and less precise, so that when you suddenly realize how very badly the fleshy overlay of "truth" fits the amalgamate bone of fact, it's too late. A lolling tongue drips a message you miss at the end of the long evening, packing the projector back up. Red in tube and chip, this "reenactment" lights up. "Darling?" The disarray evidence of a "center": spectators can't care about their own site. Wistful about authority. So (re) invent us, still weeping the solutions we came from, imagining 'things' would be fine if only a single interpretation could be *shared*, meaning *enforced*. Instead these on-going changes revealing ceaselessly shifting strategies for approach, none fully … *Have to do it again some time.* These airs equally hesitant and relentless. "Alone at last." And close? Enough. The trick is the trick is

Airs

("Scary Romantic Dark")

Jane Eyre (1934) NR Colin Clive stars in the first all-talking version of Charlotte Bronte's classic novel, one of the great romantic melodramas of all time. Raised in an orphanage and trained as a teacher, Jane Eyre (Virginia Bruce) goes to work as a governess for Edward Rochester (Clive). Inappropriately, she falls for her handsome employer, little realizing the dark, hidden secrets of his past. When Jane finally faces the truth, it may be too late.
Genre: Classic Dramas, Romance Classics, Period Pieces **Format:** DVD

Jane Eyre (1944) NR Orson Welles stars as Edward Rochester, the brooding employer of governess Jane Eyre in this adaptation of Charlotte Brontë's Gothic novel. An orphan with a tragic story herself, young Jane (Joan Fontaine) slowly frees Edward from his self-imposed prison, but his troubled past stands in the way of their burgeoning love. Directed by Robert Stevenson, this 20th Century Fox production also stars Margaret O'Brien and Agnes Moorehead.
Genre: Classic Dramas, Romance Classics, Romantic Dramas **Format:** DVD

Jane Eyre (1973) NR This BBC adaptation of Charlotte Bronte's classic novel stars Sorcha Cusack as the plucky Jane Eyre, an orphan who muddles through harsh conditions to find love in the arms of her moody employer (Michael Jayston). After being raised by an abusive aunt, young Jane survives six years in a strict, humorless school and later becomes a governess. But within the walls of her new home at Thornfield Hall, a strange and terrible secret lies in wait.

Genre: Period Pieces, Romantic Dramas, Dramas Based on the Book **Format:** DVD

Jane Eyre (1983) NR Adapted from Charlotte Brontë's gothic romance novel, this BBC miniseries tells the story of orphan Jane Eyre (Sian Pattenden and Zelah Clarke), whose early years are marked by mistreatment at the hands of her caretakers. Jane lands a governess job at the mysterious Mr. Rochester's (Timothy Dalton) estate, Thornfield, and is eventually drawn to the tortured man. But a terrible secret keeps Rochester from allowing himself to fall in love.

Genre: Romantic Dramas, Pre-20th Century Period Pieces, Dramas Based on the Book **Format:** DVD and streaming

Jane Eyre (1996) PG Director Franco Zeffirelli cemented his reputation as a faithful custodian of the classics with this adaptation of Charlotte Brontë's 1847 masterpiece *Jane Eyre*, the story of an orphan (Anna Paquin) forced to endure life at a harsh boarding school. As Jane grows into an independent, strong-willed woman (Charlotte Gainsbourg), she takes a governess job at Thornton Hall and falls in love with the estate's brooding owner, Mr. Rochester (William Hurt).

Genre: Romantic Dramas, Period Pieces, Dramas Based on the Book **This movie is:** Understated, Scary, Romantic, Dark **Format:** DVD

Jane Eyre (1997) NR Director Robert Young brings Charlotte Brontë's classic novel to life in this riveting film. After a troubled childhood, Jane Eyre (Samantha Morton) becomes a governess at Thornfield Hall, caring for young Adele (Timia Berthome). The head of the estate, Edward Rochester (Ciaran Hinds), is a brooding yet alluring older man. Jane finds herself drawn to him, but her fears and Rochester's inner torment compromise their potential romance.

Genre: Made-for-TV Movies, Dramas Based on the Book, Romantic Dramas **This movie is:** Scary, Romantic, Dark **Format:** DVD

Jane Eyre (2006) NR Toby Stephens, Francesca Annis and Ruth Wilson star in this "Masterpiece Theatre" production of the Charlotte Brontë classic about the titular governess who, resist as she may, falls deeply in love with her employer, Edward Rochester. Blissfully, he, too, feels the same way, but fate tears them apart. The wrenching tale is packed with sorrow and missed opportunities, but in the end, true romance finds a way to a satisfying, if unexpected, ending.

Genre: Romantic Dramas, Dramas Based on Classic Literature, Dramas Based on the Book **This movie is:** Sentimental, Romantic, Emotional **Format:** DVD

Jane Eyre (2011) Driven from her post at Thornfield House by her love for her brooding employer and his secret past, young governess Jane Eyre reflects on her youth and the events that led her to the misty moors in this artful adaptation of Charlotte Brontë's novel.

Genres: Drama, Romantic Dramas, Pre-20th Century Period Pieces, Dramas Based on Classic Literature, Tearjerkers, United Kingdom, Dramas Based on the Book, Blu-ray **This movie is:** Romantic, Emotional **Format:** DVD and Blu-ray

Read

"Spills out of her mother's house like a bright drop of . . ."—*don't say it!* Grandmother's raised palm commands silence: she's brought her bedside manner to the big lecture hall and she's just—that short hair really suits her—back from France. She circulates, grandmother continues, this little girl, she vanishes into the forest and reappears, setting out again on her fixed orbit through every childhood, bright flash of bravery, *look*, and innocence—so we're told—on a loop. Here she comes, there she goes. Read it again, we say sleepily, when the story is finished. Known and named for her appearance, instructed as to her behavior, our heroine crosses, again and again, that bad patch of disputed turf—accompanied by her breathless, invisible, audience. Which of us hasn't identified with her loneliness? Which of us hasn't, also, assumed the viewpoint of the wolf? Who watches her there in the woods, pausing to gather flowers, making that tired gesture of love unless it's merely a delaying tactic . . . I suspect he'd like her to be even more legible, yes? What do you think, grandmother asks. Look at the way that, in that clearing, the tall gray figure comes carefully upon the little girl, tail tucked into his pants, pretending to be a famous Botanist, or another Eminence. Pick bluebells for gratitude, he tells her, and daffodils to say *the sun shines when I am with you though a wind blows*. Ripping out a few *samples* himself, casting sidelong glances and always moving closer, he makes what he insists are only suggestions: Bring her lupines, he smirks, and maybe, *maybe*, rhododendrons. He would like to see the child in her bright garb as symbolic, a crucial part of the riveting story he's always telling himself, about himself.

It is time to take this story back, Grandmother says, or to give it back: it is time to find the *give* in this story and press ...

Start with an image: a pale young woman playing a fearful and muted game of her own invention in a house of mourning or illness, in some imposed silence. Shsssshhhh. Listen to the heavy ticking of an ancient clock, louder than her whispers: she does the dolls in different voices, mumbling endearments. Footsteps, the door opens, and she's called to don again the frayed and faded cloak, a sort of angry pink by now, much too short, told to stand on the hearthrug, asked to "make an exhibition of" herself, surrounded by her mother's friends, these more or less polite, and more than slightly plastered, adults. She has to recite again and make vivid, even entertaining, events she'd rather forget. Show ush, the distinguished critic urges, a little fuzzily, don't (hic) tell ush.

The story is not really hers at all, is it? It's the story of the woods, in some way: the story of the space between girlhood and old age, the space of a sexuality defined in terms of its social usefulness—fecundity is key, of course (yawn). The tangled edge of the forest she enters defines a space of visibility (and vulnerability) to predatory desires. In this reading, by the time she arrives at grandmother's house she *is* her grandmother (loose skin, blasted veins, wrinkles, the whole nine yards, as we say, you know—what's that flapping as I move my arm? Oh, gawd it's my arm itself), *horrible* (or so the culture is quick to inform her). But in between? In that long wander through flickering leaf light, the air thick with the scent of loam and musk? Chops are licked, wolf-whistles rend the air around her, and she is, yes, pawed—a "toothsome morsel." *I could eat you up!* And the men are, or act like, "animals." (Get pregnant and you suddenly can't find hide nor hair of 'em—scampering off, their tails between their legs, or howling at the moon, and so forth.) Dense undergrowth of clichés, perilous thicket. By the time our heroine arrives at what should be safety she understands that she has arrived at a place of invisibility (you don't exist, or only as a cautionary tale: This is what happens if you don't moisturize!). In fact, of course, she (once consumed) doesn't exist: her grandmother, as everyone knows, is a substitute. Eaten if not digested, the old woman is nothing but wolf-fuel: replaced by the image of sexual hunger, waiting in bed with a ready answer for every question, the gaze far too avid, the interest much too spookily intense.

But is anyone, in the story, really shocked by anything? Grandma clears her throat, looking out at the audience. My recollection is that they are not. Of course the fairy tale space is a dream space, in which every odd unfolding action seems connected somehow, so that strangeness flows into further, wider and wilder, strangeness with hardly a ripple and never a splash—and yet … and yet a wolf in the woods is worth two in the bed, *n'est-ce pas*? Or, a wolf in the woods should startle less, as less of an anomaly, than a wild beast in grandmother's house? Yes? Well. "Wild beast" is a courtesy: with his graduate degrees, his evening glass of lightly oaked chardonnay, his high, gleaming forehead and those expensively maintained teeth, his passion for first editions or something like that, his monographs on Eliot or Yeats … —*eh bien*, beastly but not in fact a beast, *hélas*. I say nothing against actual wolves! But we should, this once, remark the odd tendency to read the dialogue as a logical response to chaos and danger! Look: the door swings open on a house in disarray, broken crockery, bloodstains maybe, and (in the bedroom) something decidedly weird about the scene … lipstick smeared on the furry jowls, the heavy drag, the emphatic denial of grandmother's absence. Even if we can inhabit, briefly, the POV of the predator, we must unfailingly return to our inside knowledge (so to speak) of the situation of the powerless: we meet a wolf, and again we meet a wolf … and we are, and here grandmother's voice takes on a tone of exasperation, we are repeatedly asked to believe that the very lack of knowledge that endangers us might keep us safe! But who here hasn't been deceived and devoured? Grandmother gently asks, removing her glasses. She is so patient with our urgent desire for a story that will run again and again rigidly along the well-laid tracks, she's understanding about our desire for the feeling of forward movement confined by a reassuring structural stasis. She confesses that she too … I myself have a memory of wanting to hear the same song over and over, lifting and putting the needle back down on the glossy black of the spinning vinyl disc—that technology (Oh my dears, we called them "records"! Hilarious!) now chic because out-dated: perhaps its meaning will be as mysterious someday as a stone tablet etched with hieroglyphics … We want to memorize the words that seem so fine to us, don't we? And maybe it's true that we need to go through a controlled version of the trauma again—in order to survive it? But let's stop here and consider our heroine's situation for a moment: stalled on the threshold of a dangerous encounter, in which the password will literally allow the speaker to pass, to pass away, to be consumed, to meet, as we say, her death. Of course we wish she were stronger, braver, smarter, faster or just … ready for this. It is our constant wish.

I wasn't fooled, she asserts, inaudibly at first but, then, seeming quite poised for one so young, speaking distinctly into the microphones—flanked by her handlers and image consultants—*not for an instant!*

I was just noticing how smart the fairy tale is about the steps that could lead us to normalize a situation both strange and potentially catastrophic. In stress situations, it turns out (unless we have imagined what could happen and what to do in "the event of a possible disaster"), the first reaction is stasis and denial—manifested as shock. What stands out about Little Red Riding Hood's confrontation with the wolf is how on top of it she is, or could seem, anyway: able at once to articulate her observation of difference. So, we could see her as intrepid and bold, or cool, as we say now, but we might also, shifting the framework a little, see her as having been raised in a madhouse: educated to debate wolves, or trained (like an airline stewardess) to pretend that things are just fine when they are not fine, not at all fine, not in the least. Really! Imagine it: that's a wolf in my grandmother's bed!?! What do you do? Let me tell you: you open the door, you see there's a wolf in granny's queen-sized water bed, and you haul your ass *outta* there—fast. Being afraid was the right reaction in that situation, the analyst tells her, later, when she wants to go over the incident again. "Maybe I could've …" No. No: you were too late. It's not your fault. The amazing part is that you stayed there so long, given the circumstances. Was the child intrepid, a real risk-taker, or just brought up to put the social conventions before her own life? It's a question we need to ask. Maybe she stopped behind the mall, before entering the woods, to sniff some glue or pop one of the Vicodin she hopes her mom won't miss. I'm serious! It might be terror, but when I replay the conversation she has with the wolf, near the end of the story, Little Red Riding Hood sounds ... high.

The woods? Let's go back to the woods, the forest, the designated wilderness area—crisscrossed by subtle and less subtle paths, deep grooves of dragged logs, traces of fear and hunger: winding indications of the passage of first the rabbit and then the fox, or some larger dog. Patterns of pleasure: the hiking trail, the print of boots and stick, indications of prudence: the fire road's wide gap ... marked and remarked. The spoor, the discarded beer can, the ring of blackened stones holding a circle of ash. And who we were, to ourselves and to each other, constantly renegotiated, what we meant ...

Then back, go back once more, then: do you think you can talk about it now?

The critic, I mean critter, in bed with the covers pulled up to the matted fur of his jowls. Bright-eyed, faking innocent attention the way a woman no longer in love fakes an orgasm. "The reader," he says, casually—explaining what's wrong with her work—displaying his enviably easy assumption that there is a definite article audience, and that we, or rather he, knows exactly what they want. He mostly wants everything to stay just exactly as it is, except that it should be easier to get what *he* wants. Which is more of what he has, of course. What he likes:

his taste. Our hunger dwindles on the unchanging fare he'll allow as he works mostly to mask the costs of his desires, which appall him? Which might appall us—those of us left—were we given time to total them up. His mouth goes liquid as he imagines pouncing on that fresh morsel wrapped in her scarlet cloak. *As if already covered in blood* he sings to himself. But if he springs too soon his claws will close on nothing, or he'll be stopped, and humiliated, while if he leaps too late, if she's too near the door ("Come closer child . . .") she'll escape. It's better, more intelligent, to just lie there, trying not to tremble with lust and rage. (Why should I defer my pleasures, he whines, why why why, when life is so . . . brief!) But why does he tremble? Someone must ask! After all he usurped the past, completely, or trimmed it to fit his prejudices, got Stein off the curriculum entirely, substituted Hemingway as the truly "nourishing" dish—nourishing whom? For what? He turns his head toward the opening door, his eyes wide. He looks, the little girl thinks, almost frightened, in his poor imitation of loving, in his stiff and over-dramatic acting out of what he supposes intimacy might be like. Of course he despises what he finds to be not only *difficult* but, for his purposes, meaningless. And the air in the room is strangely thick, damp, a deep lush tainted sweetness the child associates with visits to the butcher's shop.

She pauses for a moment and then pushes open the scratched front door, noticing the broken lock, and—once inside—stops in the doorway to the bedroom, trying to pretend nothing's really too different, though the air stinks of fear and musk and there's a streak of what looks like blood on the sleeve of the nightdress. Fine, it's fine, everything's . . . She employs the dull cunning or cunning dullness born of years (already) of dealing with tricky, more or less threatening, adults. She freezes on the threshold, sticks her gum on the side of the basket and her voice has a tightness as she begins, almost mechanically, to try to both talk him down and lull herself: let's pretend there's nothing wrong here … It's hard to watch, isn't it? Of course we wish she had a gun, we ardently hope she's just stalling for time, checking those freaky eyes for the first indication of the intended pounce, wondering *Where the fuck is my backup?!*

Well come in girl, he croaks in his nasty quivering cover of an old lady voice, his unsteady contemptuous falsetto, a terrible imitation, actually, a joke. Don't stand there letting the flies in, he creaks (shut the door, shut your mouth), don't gawp! There's a draft. In the version of the story he likes his students to read (and write) she marries the woodsman, goes off to her isolated life in that dim and drafty log cabin, loses touch with friends who've lost a sense of what to say to each new bruise and "accident," concerned but uncertain of how to respond to every brisk assurance that things at home are *fine*. Thanks! Everyone knows he drinks, everyone, so they claim now, told her not to … Don't do it. He's twice your age, they say they said, and I know you're grateful, but … They insist, now, that they warned her. But it would have made her grandmother so happy to know she was married or as we used to say, "provided for …"—or so she, as he tells us to tell ourselves ("this is what the story means," "this is the most important part of the story"), tells herself. For that is one of his primary contentions: if she's in trouble now (and she does, in fact, seem to be in trouble), it's because of the stories she told herself without his say so. *She wanted it.*

"What … uh … big eyes," I begin, at a loss, speaking very carefully: trying not to seem at all surprised by what I'm seeing. *It's fine.* But the first expression of awareness that there is indeed some crucial difference between what I see and what I expected to see sets the critter going with attempted explanations meant to lead (step by step, read my lips, it's the narrative, stupid) to my death and immediate joining of my grandmother in that bloated stomach where what isn't to be read or seriously considered anymore wetly sleeps. I'm meant to vanish down there, either almost completely ignored (like everything by Laura Riding Jackson) or lingering only as memory, admired, perhaps, but rarely taught (like H. D.'s *Helen in Egypt*). "The better to …, the better to …": it's astonishing, the way each aspect of the substitution, once remarked, is explained as a *means*, as if I needed to be reminded of the importance of usefulness. But these are just tools, child, the wolf condescends to explain (snappish, like, duh, in his deep voice): eyes, teeth, et cetera … I need them for certain tasks! At first the uses seem reasonable and benign and then they become more dubious, at last revealing their essentially nefarious … But of course I'm not comparing my situation to that of the victims of the … it's just that this efficient progression from carefully normalized danger toward unthinkable disaster has me thinking of that colorized flash of soft vermillion isolated in the dreary black and white of *Schindler's List*. A despicable emphasis, tacky as the upsurge of strings in the over-wrought soundtrack, the director's way of making sure we *feel* the Holocaust? Six million people were killed and one of them was—wait for it—An Innocent Little Girl? A fairy tale character … What's that armband for, grandma, why are you wearing those big black boots? How can you go on citing Heidegger and de Man at this point? And

Nietzsche, did he really write that stuff about women, Grandma? You told me you were part of the *Resistance* …

Her plan was to stop off at granny's, deliver the meds, cheer her up a bit if possible, and then (the large, heavy basket actually mostly packed with rope, water, food, a roll of toilet paper, some plastic bags, and blankets) climb one of the old growth trees in the grove recently purchased by the lumber company—in what had formerly been a protected area of the designated wilderness. The irony of having to be *rescued* by a representative of the company she was hoping to thwart puts her teeth on edge every time her grandma talks about how nice he was, how handsome, how strong, etc., so boyish, so polite! Despite the fact that they've been dating for awhile now, and are starting to plan a wedding in either what's left of the grove or a clear cut, depending on the date, she still has this image of herself alone high up in the branches, her hair tangled, her eyes huge, framed against the foliage, a little pale from hunger and lack of sleep …

Oh it's an old and unproductive wolf, grandma continues, lolling and drooling in his cork-lined room, beginning to sleep when he reads his own assertions ("this method seems self-indulgent"), reciting again his objections lest he forget. He's grayish or balding, he's scrawny or running to fat, the nice years of feasting on the tender admiring glances of coeds, and sometimes the coeds themselves, long past. The time of "promise" distant. She sighs and shakes her head—maybe we'll never be able to really understand what it means, to be able to see yourself as the potential heir of everything, to believe there's nothing you can't have—it's a sort of magical condition, quite out of imagining, really, despite all the novels and memoirs which trace the arc of this entitlement and the reactions of those who (almost but not quite successful, or not to the extent they could hope) become ferocious, even deadly, in their inevitable disappointment.

In fact, but the young woman only comes to understand this much later, under analysis, her grandmother must've been sleeping with both the woodsman and the wolf (well, we assume on different nights) for several years. Privacy is a really good reason to live in the forest—that and being close to that strip of bars by the Interstate (The Alibi, The Log Cabin, The Whistle Stop). They had some fun. The girl almost walked in on them once: the door creaked & granny cried out "Who's there?!" "It's me," she said—hearing giggles and an urgent, whispered, *Shush*. Oh he ate her up all right! Granny? Every time I went to see her she was in bed, empty bottles in the filthy living room, cigarette burns in the dirty sheets—no wonder mom kept saying granny wasn't feeling well enough to visit. Red laughs and tosses back the rest of the bourbon, reaches out for her cigarettes (though she'll wait to light up in the parking lot); you know what? It's taken some time to admit it, but, actually … Granny was probably feeling great.

Not everything was ruined, she notes with satisfaction, folding items to go to the thrift shop. Here's a dainty lace night-cap, for instance, with just a single jagged rip along one edge.

There is a draft.

Let it be understood that I only intended to console you, or that I understood your desire to be consoled and … —what could be wrong with that?

She pauses on the threshold. "We're out of the woods now" is a cliché, a way of framing a commitment to a particular sense (sight) and our desire to see clearly, to see all around us. It's an old image for fear, the woods, fear of being hurt or lost. Herr Doctor Wolfson was concerned about publishing the version he saw: he thinks there should be more about the death. The images should be wetter. The part where she talks about how he put his paws all over her—that's the "heart" of the story, he insists. He explains again that *the reader's* hunger is for a page-turner, a book that can be assigned to as many classes as possible, literature surveys, for instance, in the same semester as *The Sun Also Rises* … —oh, I am way "off track" as we say, or far from the beaten track (if closer to the beating). He dismisses theory easily, has nothing but a fine impatience for the "experimental," reminds us that he waited long enough before he launched his own career as a poet. But why do we say "neck of the woods"—I've never understood that. Are the woods to be seen as a body? A girl no longer a girl, old enough to be a grandmother herself, stands in the doorway, a cloak too short in a color too bright billowing around her gray hair, her tired eyes, the puckered blotchy skin of her sad face. The sign in the window says *Soins du Visage*. Come in come in he barks and then he makes it softer, tries for the sweetness of a "granny" in an advertisement: shut the door behind you child, there's a draft … Or C'mon out of that draft, these old bones need heat, and so forth (Grandmother's house is ideally a trailer in Pensacola or a condo in Vegas); What have you brought your poor old sick … (was that a hiccup of self-pity or a belch?) (the actual grandmother—swallowed in a single gulp—sitting badly on his stomach). Now come closer dear to your poor old sick granny who loves narrative poetry, he murmurs fretfully, poetry as transparent as the window the speaker (someone like us, he'll assert—blithely ignoring the facts) looks through, more interested in exploring his or her own sensitivity than any of the limited (from that vantage) subjects. "I looked out the window and I saw … and then I thought … and then I felt … ," and hey presto a comparison, and epiphany: one split second of being the owl or … wolf? Come here child, come just a little bit closer … —"You have to realize," he insists, "how little a dry, cerebral, splintering method can communicate about its subject—or even how inadequately it can communicate, in bodied form, what its subject is …"

Note the frost of white hairs along the muzzle, Grandma says sternly, standing over the deflated carcass: look at the length (where the gums have receded) of those yellow teeth! She smiles, a little breathless and damp but otherwise fine. She urges us to consider the issue of sexuality and social value, to triangulate the question of the *wild*, looking at the way the child and the crone are aligned with the untamed beast. Child and crone are not yet or no longer domesticated by a "sexuality" which takes its place as one of a number of disciplining procedures, extending the possibility of serving as mother and wife.

She can do this, she thinks, though in fact she never got over the deep hurt of the long ago rape. She could have lost her mind—for a time there, in the clinic, it looked as if she might … such a deep silence she kept, all through the treatment. It wasn't until her sister said, "I know you're in there …"—but the young woman who *came out on the other side*, as we say, not fixed but functional, is (among so much else) wary and easily exasperated, though she tries, when she can, to hide that lack of patience. Scar and surgical thread, it's the red or read wound itself that travels, stitching together the edges of that gap between the mother's kitchen and the grandmother's bed, the stretch of her own sexuality, crossing the perilous wilderness (which is, under current EPA rulings, itself at risk) to bring the disparate parts of her life into contact. The girl is as far from birth as her grandmother is (under normal circumstances) from death. This suturing must be repeated: the story is read and reread and rereread. The eyes of the auditors flutter—they know the ending … you don't have to stay awake if you know the ending, if you recognize one of the most likely endings as it approaches, arms full of flowers that speak to us.

Read it again, we murmur, again. Read it. The shadow of the ax falls across the drawn shade of the window behind the bed as the room echoes with the fearsome words in which the deception is dropped: *The better to eat you with!* Though that charged Q & A remains important, we'll always wish our heroine had said something like "What the fuck are *you* looking at!" or even just "As if!" Something tough, proving she's no fool, she's a survivor, even if it reminds us that she wasn't brought up well—if she had to stay at all, if she had to speak. *Fuck you,* we imagine her scoffing (and we imagine ourselves cheering her on: say it!), *you pathetic little shit.* And then everything should happen at once: the window's glass crashing in, an ax swinging down, a spray of blood fanning up around the leering jaws and lolling tongue, and the glee in the wolf's eyes extinguished. At last. Then Red, with a bad case of Stockholm syndrome and her lifetime membership in the Sierra Club, crying on the floor beside the body: "You … you could have just *trapped* him … you could've released him in [sniff] Wyoming or … something …" Ah, my dear, my dear … *this* breed, Grandma gently laughs, stepping away from the podium, is in no danger of going extinct! *I know you're in there.* From its opening chords to be able to say exactly how the song goes and, so, to be able to sing along: "The sun shines when I am with you, though a wind blows." *Bite me!* Once once once …

Trust

(Corps à corps)

Even now, 41 years later, if I think of him his name comes back (both his names) immediately and easily: gliding up like air-filled buoys from an opaque and then translucent depth, flashing to the surface like markers for a wreck or trap, or floats from a storm-torn net. "Mr. Jerome." "Theodore." (I never called him that but knew it: "Mr. Theodore Jerome.") So many other names I've lost, so many new names these days I just can't seem to take in, no matter how often they're said (as if there's a certain resistance)—there's something more than a bit disturbing about the clarity of my memory for both of the names of a man I never think about or think I never think about.

His name, his names, and then the chalky mint on his breath because he scented his breath for me, as he might have done (for all I know) for any of his students. And so perhaps his wife was not disturbed or surprised as she watched (or if she noticed) his preparations for my visit, putting the breath mint on his tongue, mouth gaping beneath the gray military moustache. The full memory isn't, at first, altogether present: making the notes for this essay I thought "breath mint" and then *or whatever kind of mint it was*, but in fact, now I think of it he kept them in his pocket: he offered me one, I took it. There's the gleam of the blue wrapping? You don't need to trust me: I hardly know whether to trust myself. I'll never know what his wife thought: if she knew but managed not to know, or managed not to know but knew—you know—all those possible variations. I doubt that they're still alive and I don't know if they had children. I was 9, he was 60, something; his hands, though I do not want to get to his hands too quickly, shook … with age? That was what I thought.

The place was Montecito, California and the year was 1967, which means the town wasn't yet a suburb of Hollywood but a retreat from the entertainment business: a sleepy, artsy, well-heeled progressive, or even hippie, oasis. There was a lot of money but it wasn't gaudy: a lot of it was old and much of it went into Culture. When the I. Magnin catalogue came out with the velvet smoking dress that cost $800.00 one of my grand-mother's friends, a long-time I. Magnin shopper, sent them her cut-up store credit card with a curt note: "It's wicked to charge that much for clothes!" Money at that point in that place had some other uses than to advertise itself—or perhaps it just had to whisper to make itself heard. And we were poor—not just comparatively but welfare-powdered-eggs-for-breakfast poor— yet could live there too, somehow: half a block from the railroad tracks which meant another half a block from Miramar beach. The glass floats the Japanese used for their nets rolled up on the sand among bits of abalone shell and stranded jellyfish and gobs of tar. Humphrey Road. There are addresses of mine I've forgotten, that one comes back at once with an almost inaudible pop. And the names of our neighbors, other neighbors, and family friends are there too, but I won't, as they surface, say them: this isn't a nice story. I've thought about telling it but I've never wanted to tell it, and there's no reason to involve anyone who doesn't have to be there, no one who isn't already swim-ming in whatever it is that kept me silent.

Earlier tonight I was reading *Walden,* and when Thoreau said
"I never knew, and never shall know, a worse man than myself" I
paused. I liked the phrase, its implications, and then wondered
for a heartbeat do I …? Oh yes, I do: I did, once. I suppose,
in saying so, I am less aligned with Thoreau than I am with a
younger generation of Americans who—so a recent newspa-
per article tells me—steal and cheat in increasing numbers and
know of no one better than themselves. "Everyone I know is
worse than me," they are cited as saying. Well, I know a man
worse than myself or I did know … And then I get that giggle
that comes from reading the endless male writers who address
themselves to an audience they assume will be endlessly male:
as I am a *woman* I must certainly be one of the worst *men* I
know? I was reading *Walden* because my friend who owns the
local used bookstore was asked to come deal with the stored
and forgotten effects of a dead English professor: he brought
back this lovely edition I couldn't resist. I was reading *Walden*
because I bought it as a gift for someone and then thought it
might be a gift for someone with whom I was suddenly in love;
but I had never read the book. And this story or anecdote or
confession had come to mind as I tried to make sense of my
decision not to stay the night with someone who wanted me
to stay: why not just … If I slept with him, he said, I might
make him forget someone else. So the past became present or
deepened the present: I do, I know a man who … Among the
dust-thick boxes of books in the storage unit, my friend told
me, was a collection of pornographic magazines from the 1960s.
"I'll deal with that," he quoted the owner of the storage unit
as saying, decisively, the same phrase he used when my friend

opened (the other anomaly among boxes of books and books and books) a deep carton of sterling silver flatware. I'll deal with that.

It was something I wondered whether I should tell you. I never know how much it matters, to me first of all. It matters and it doesn't matter, too much and too little (I could say, like everything else), and I wondered whether it was something I should tell you (not the dread phrase "we need to talk," but a slightly revised version: "I need to talk"). There's something I want you to know—there's something I never want you to know. *There's something* … —spooky phrase all by itself, halted like that: air in it.

I think he unhooks his screen door: he's been waiting for me (how did he hide that fact from his wife or did he bother to hide it?). Was he in the back room sometimes, arranging equipment, or was he watching TV? Was she also watching? Did she come to the door herself sometimes, his wife (whose name I don't recall) drying her hands on a tea towel, or the edge of her apron; am I making this up? Was her hair dyed red? Was she cold or reserved, was she sweet, did she welcome me or ignore me? Was she part of it? Of course she is part of it, somehow, as are we all: Mr. Jerome, my mother and stepfather, my younger brother who is there and isn't, busy with intricate boy adventures, my father, 900 miles away with his new lady, as we said back then, my second stepmother … all of us part of the mild afternoon and my standing on the slab of concrete that functions as a little porch for that bungalow behind our house, waiting to be let in by Mr. or Mrs. Jerome for one of the private fencing lessons which is not going to cost my parents anything. An amazing and wonderful thing, because Mr. Jerome is, in the parlance, a fencing *master*, teaching fencing (to the rich and the children of the rich) in downtown Santa Barbara, where he has a studio, a school, with his name on it. Let me be very clear: teaching fencing is how he earns his living, and it is his passion, also, so we understand? Surely that is, also, part of this: his passion for the art is part of what makes explicable the fact that he wants to give lessons—for nothing—to his neighbor's daughter? How else do we make sense of it or how soon do I make another sense of this desire on his part? And whose desire was it—or how much was mine (my fault)? There's that.

Starting to write this I spoke to more than one friend about this breaking of so long a silence. But, and this began to be almost funny, it turns out that a story I think everyone I'm close to already knows, is—as I only discover by saying "I'm writing about …"—something I've told almost no one … or almost everyone forgot? I kept assuming that though I couldn't write about it I'd already … somehow, somewhere … What keeps happening is that I want to talk about the writing ("a breakthrough"), but I find myself trying to explain the events to someone feeling for me as a person, or, even, as a little girl. "I'm sorry that happened to you" is hard for me to hear. But, "You'll have to take fencing lessons," when my friend said that, with her wise laugh, I knew she was right. Yes. But first this work of memory and language, the effort to move back into a part of my life so long shut off.

He is French or they both are? That his wife is German seems to come to me slowly and vaguely and remains uncertain. How focused I must have been on him. He is French: indisputable accent, indisputable military mustache and (oh god, I had forgotten this) a black or midnight blue beret. Jesus. I had forgotten that. Piercing eyes, but I cannot (I am relieved and anxious to tell you) tell you if they were bright or dark. Excellent, military bearing, the back, as they say, ramrod straight. Up close his eyes were rheumy: I recall his few white hairs and "palsied hand," the bad smell from his body or his clothes, smell of age and of that airless house. "Bad" smell: that's the nine year-old coming back, she wrote that, she's caught there, thinking that: bad, ick, wanting to turn her head away, wanting out of that windowless (it comes to me, it begins to arrive) back room. There's a chiaroscuro to the images as they return, as if they are badly developed, there's a stark intensity of dark and light. Something like terror coming as the memory opens: windowless room, glaring light dangling on a cord, I want out of there—I know it (this bare room lit by a single bulb)—isn't safe. But I believe I didn't know that at first.

Mr. Jerome taught fencing somewhere downtown, pleasant, airy, the top of a building we passed (I saw the windows: was I ever inside?), expensive and public. It was (and is, no doubt—I haven't been back in some time) the kind of town where people took dancing lessons and fencing lessons and took their children to such lessons and people had horses and rode, "to hounds" for all I know, for when I read books about gorgeous and grand country houses it is the mansions of Montecito that fill out the details of what I read, and why not? Even then film crews came to town for just that purpose. But they might not have been so well off either, the Jeromes, now I think of it, despite the downtown studio (or because of its costly rent?). They lived in a bungalow tucked behind another house, up a dirt driveway, half a block from the railroad tracks, behind the high gooseberry hedge, near the creek. Maybe they were paying off a lawsuit? It's not an impossibility, I think—or so I would like to think?

What's the initial conversation? How does the subject come up? Mr. Jerome offers to give me fencing lessons, for free, after school, at his house. Do I ask for lessons? When I recall this, meaning when I have recalled this, meaning when I do and do not recall this, I never come as far as this: did I ask? Did I ask, did I plead, did I say I really really really … I think that's possible. I was what we called a tomboy: the usual toys for girls my age, like the baby doll that peed and closed its eyes, seemed absurdly tedious—I literally could not imagine how it would be fun to play at taking care of this sodden blinking blob of awkward plastic. I was excited by race cars and pop music, *Dark Shadows, Bewitched, Batman,* and *The Wild Wild West*: the idea of learning how to sword fight (for so I must've imagined it) would've thrilled me. I've never admitted that. Whenever I get close enough to this even to say "fencing lessons—for free," my rage starts, my distancing defensive fury: was there any sense in my parents' heads at all, I want to ask. (It's a question that was answered early, but one I kept wanting—waiting for a better answer—to ask.) Was there some missing part of this bargain that would help it make some other sense? An offer to barter (for sometimes it worked like that for my parents, the complicated negotiations they made with a world they could never afford, they never moved as equals in, they always felt diminished by)

I've forgotten … I can't ask my mother, who is the only one I could ask: I'm afraid a direct question would overwhelm her with guilt (only the slowly achieved certainty that she resolutely ignores my 'career' makes it safe to pose the question here: I am—*vis à vis* my mother—more alone with this essay than I was with my 'diary,' as a 'troubled' adolescent). What the fuck were they thinking? That's the shape it takes, my despair at their failure to be canny, savvy about the ways the world actually worked, to be careful (care-full): they loved me, they love me, they … I have tried all my life to be smarter than that. *What the fuck* is the bugle blast of my furious impatience. I wanted to be smart enough (fast enough) to be safe and to keep those I love safe. But this was before the long negotiations with sexuality really began, or this was before I, as we say, represented myself.

I think I recall that my mother was giddy about the good deal we were getting, but I could be projecting that. Bargains thrilled her: getting something valuable for cheap (which was all we could afford or mostly more than we could afford) seemed something like a sign of grace. If my parents were suspicious about this at all I have forgotten it. Was I? Was there worry and if there was, what did we do to allay it? Was it just assumed that it was okay because his wife was there, after all, in the house? What about my Grandmother: did she worry, did she know, or did this seem just another aspect of her own wonderful luck? I'm decades too late to ask this question or any question of her (who were they, all those faces in the box of photographs left in her closet?); I'll never know the names of the family members she'd cut herself off from, my Grandmother, or lost track of by marrying an artist, by entering a life that revolved around art. I think I was excited and nervous (I was going to learn to fence!)—learning anything made me nervous and I was, you should know, utterly lousy at almost every sport: clumsy and terrified equally of flying objects, competition, and any kind of judgment. Timid and fierce, awkward and energetic: that's a start to the portrait; skinny and blond and pink-cheeked. And one afternoon after school I presented myself at the door of my neighbor's house and began to be instructed in those ritualized gestures (a stylized, choreographed version of violence) that involve the body and mind and have (as in music, or poetry) the power to startle and thrill in their rearrangement.

Lunge, parry: I am only, for now, going to use the little bit of language that comes back. "A little language, such as lovers use," as Virginia Woolf puts it (in another context), later I'll look more words up (I haven't thought about the jargon since, I never *ever* again tried to learn to fence). I loved it: the ritual, the costume, the white jacket, the strange screen masks, the sword, no, "foil": the "foil." The one I liked and chose and owned (we purchased that, I think, we must've, as I got to keep it) had a "Belgian" grip. Salute. Swish of metal in air, downward, deliberately harmless: a greeting before we start. Someone unhooks the screen door, on the latch, or later (as the days draw in) opens a shut door and then unhooks the screen in the early dark. How long does this go on? How deep into the instruction did it come, his first suggestion that we "rest"? Each move he made would have been balanced between his desire to touch me and the concern not to scare me off or make me make some noise that would alert his wife: was it like taming something wild? I've done that: I know how to defer what it is I want while waiting for whatever it is (squirrel or feral cat, for instance) to come round to the idea that you are the source of something they want. "Let's rest," he suggested, and though I wasn't tired I didn't protest. He was old: it didn't surprise me at first that he wanted to rest. I think I may have tried sometimes, later, to say no, to say no I'm not tired yet, trying to work within the pretext. By the end I understood the code … at the start I didn't.

I know a man worse than myself, I said, and I wasn't speaking of a former president … —there's the voice I put on and can't take off: the tough, smart (ass) voice meant to warn whoever comes near that I can take care of myself … I had to take care of myself. Well we all do, so what. It was a little early. What I began to wonder as I wrote about this ("at last") is this: at what point did I know I would have to pay for the lessons and in what coin? At what point did I know that I was going to have to pay for the lessons by letting him touch me—and at what point, having realized that, did I say (not out loud, of course, not 'in so many words') *yes*.

There's a tall (twice as high as I was then) gooseberry hedge between the two houses, and two scraps of tough bright lawn I cross in the early dark. The houses are so close and I move so fast our back door is banging shut behind me as I knock at Mr. & Mrs. Jerome's house. He pops a mint in his mouth and goes to the door or she does, drying her hands on a little towel because she is already in the kitchen getting their dinner ready? There's a scent of food? The house is too warm, it's stuffy, there's a television on, I think, that flickering light and a small lamp I rush past to the back where we practice. I arrive in the white cotton jacket I have purchased, holding my foil and my mask, I think. And for a time we practice. I am trying now— but I am also afraid to try—to feel what he is feeling, whose heart I am trying (with the bandaged tip of that narrow length of springy steel) to touch. Was it a calculated risk? A weakness they both knew about, he and his wife? There is no Lolita to this: I have barely any tits or ass now, back then I was perfectly flat. I suppose I mean to say, meaning I mean you to hear me saying, there was no seduction: I wasn't tired or rather even if I did sometimes get tired I didn't ever want to "rest."

The Baton Rouge Fencing Club meets in the wide grey lino-leum-floored gym of a Korean church. One of my colleagues is a coach there and, with his encouragement, on the night of the last class of the semester I show up. I've only said I used to fence and that I am interested—no more than that. My friend lends me his creased, well-worn, garb: the jacket rust-stained from lying among his foils in the Louisiana damp, the darkened glove so molded by use it seems to have a hand already in it as he holds it out for me to take. I was afraid the mere sight of the gear would devastate me: I'd wondered if I'd have to leave in tears at the sight of … well, I didn't know what. Instead there's a sense of familiarity: I know these items, I know what they are for … though I had forgotten the intimate strap that pulls the point of the jacket (polyester and not the stiff cotton I recall) down between the legs, and I didn't remember the way the mask (ad-justed for me) locked down under the chin, the padded "bib" pressed to the vulnerable throat. What shocks me, what I didn't expect, is how comfortable I feel outfitted like this. "We usu-ally," my friend says, "just push the mask back to the top of our heads when we're not actually … because it gets so hot …" But I leave the mask down, I wander about the room in full regalia (not unlike, it comes to me today, the Dustin Hoffman character in *The Graduate*, in his diving gear): I am in another element. What I feel, fully dressed for fencing, is the opposite of what I had expected: I feel *safe*. I hadn't expected it, but I might have? Of course he never molested me (oh, that word) when I had the mask on, when I was holding the foil, when I was—in other words—fully suited in the trappings of our shared practice.

His sticky, rough lips. The chalky mint of his mouth on mine, the bristle of that stiff grey mustache. I have never written this: barely thought it. His liver-spotted hands clutching, I wrote (in the first draft), that child close. Her. Me. I am not what he is holding, I wrote, to reassure myself. "Is this story going where I think it's going," another friend asks, glancing away, as I begin to speak of this writing, of what it is I am at last writing about. I can't tell you the exact moment, but I know that when I understood what the cost was I said okay, I can pay for these lessons like this, I can ignore and then (later) I can endure this. And so I entered a life where people could touch me without touching me, a life in which I knew how, in almost any grasp (or so I thought), to vanish? Or so I thought? I imagine I had already entered that life, even by nine: people say so casually to children "Don't run away! You have to let …" The family member who wants to hug the child gets to hug the child even if the child doesn't like it. There's something there for me—some memory I refuse to pull at—leave it at this: I didn't like being touched by those I didn't love, including family members or friends of the family too rarely encountered for real connection? It was a very touchy-feely (so the language goes) place, California, in those days, and there were lots of strangers who were suddenly intimate and then not, and I had to hug and let myself be hugged by those who—like my first stepmother—didn't actually like me very much. (I think I tried to feel something for that woman besides fear, but I'm not sure I managed it.) I'm not sure whose hold I relaxed in, though I recall (from high school onward and at least into my thirties) thinking, when I was in trouble, *hold me just please hold me*, as if to be wrapped in another's arms would make everything right.

When Thoreau makes his claim he is of course referring us to the work of looking within in order to see more clearly without. If he brags, as he'll say elsewhere in the book, "for humanity," he also confesses for it: we need to know our own hearts. But he is speaking before the birth and death of some astonishingly terrible men, and also closing his eyes to a great deal of what was, if not "evil" (I hate that simplistic label), then horribly, demonstrably, wrong in humanity by his own epoch. He uses slavery as a metaphor too often, and dismisses the Irish in sentences that reveal his complete confidence in our shared understanding of their many faults. As for New England, well, "the witches are all hung," he announces, with the air of one mentally dusting off his hands. I think, I joked to a friend after starting *Walden*, he'd be an awful lover: I'd kick Thoreau out of bed, I laughed, for Baudelaire, despite the syphilis. How grim to watch that anxious Yankee "score," as we used to say, teeth gritted as he totaled his accounts! So I put it on again: a certain toughness. With some completely unforgettable exceptions it's been mostly a farce, my sex life. Summer sang in me all right but too often in the churning senseless rhythms of a pop hit as the headboard thunked against the wall for the requisite three minutes. The body was there, but the heart, the mind ... So much pressure in the deep water of the desire of others, all around that body, such endless attentions and so many of those mean, so many dangerous; so much to parry, so little space to find out what I wanted or might learn to look for, ask for. Trust? Everything at "that tender age of becoming," as Carole Maso puts it, in another context: an age that, in some ways, never stops.

I recognized at once the rhythms of the footwork the intermediate class was practicing in the gym, and the language also: "Balestra," *Balestra*: Stomp st st stomp, stomp st st stomp— the beat came back, and though I couldn't find the footwork at first, the stance returned in minutes. I wondered and was going to ask someone but what do I do with my left hand? Then I felt it gradually float up beside my head as if I were possessed ... —I knew exactly where it went and how the fingers ... But remember to throw your arm back in the lunge, my colleague admonished, and a phrase came back to me, neutral, not in the voice of my teacher though they were his words, and I repeated them aloud. Oh yes, I said, to *narrow the target*.

Where I left her so long ago: that nine year old girl, in the arms of the fencing master, working, now, his quivering hand over the waistband of her pants, and then after searching the outside of her elasticized god-awful white (why do I care? Somehow I care ...) underwear inserting one trembling finger into the cleft of her hairless ... I stop there, writing this. When at last I found a way to say something about what was going on and why I wanted to stop the lessons, someone in the family might have used the word "pervert." Now we would say pedophile, perhaps? Now he would, if his offense were known, be registered: my parents could look him up or bond with other concerned parents to try to make him feel it would be better to live somewhere else? "I do, I know a man worse than …," I think, finding my way back through old ways: "Mr. Jerome is a dirty old man." Some months after the lessons had stopped, I—emboldened by a friend's presence—wrote that message on a piece of paper and put it in the mailbox next to ours. He found it as he was meant to (I knew he checked his mail and when) and then he sort of chased or followed us down the street as we chanted it at him: "a dirty old man!" There'd been a movie with such a character, or my parents or one of their friends had said that? Somehow I'd got hold of the label and could use it. He couldn't run fast enough to catch us, but it seemed a great risk: my heart pounding as I walked swiftly backward up the tree-lined street, eyes locked on him, "You are!" "Come here!" "No!" What did his wife …, what did the neighbors think? Why is it that that shouted accusation still seems to disappear or almost disappear into a silence, intimate as if I'd whispered it?

When I ask my mother—and this, on a recent visit, is as close as I will get—about that time, she remembers what a nice neighborhood that was, what a lovely place to live.

I know how to move forward (*advance*, the familiar word), I know how to retreat. I can see now (though no one touches another person in the wide bright gym of the church) that there might be a context in which you would reach out, to adjust the angle of a lifted arm, say—perhaps it started like that? Or am I making that up? Am I trying to forgive him here? I'm trying to know my own heart ("for lack," as Roland Barthes will say, quoting Balzac, "of a better word"), that heart which, if it is not exactly my body, is in no way (as I thought I could make it) separate from my body. That I would become a teacher myself is part of this, I suspect. What comes to me in the Baton Rouge gym—what I had never thought of—as I watch one coach watch and attempt to adjust 10 or so students, is the value (there is no other word) of the instruction I got. *I had*, I say to my colleague, coming as close as I'll come to trying to say what it is I'm doing here, *private lessons*. My voice a little funny on "private." The lessons, I find myself saying (alone and almost aloud, later), were real. The lessons were real: there's something expressed in the dumb phrase that moves me as nothing else does— … do you understand a little? That he communicated this skill and knowledge, that he was a teacher, and took those lessons seriously, that, in fact, we both did … *that* understanding is the first thing, in all of this, that makes me want to weep.

I thought I had to endure it, and for some time I endured it. He slithered a wad of muscular and minty tongue past my lips. I kept my teeth shut at first and then, I think, he made it clear I should open them, too. It's partially that I'm a little stupid about the body but it's also that I was so young: all the gestures lacked context. The space between my legs he's finally (there were stages) worked his fingers to and is fumbling at is where the pee comes out: I would have read or may have been told that there are other aspects to that particular place on my body but such is, so far, my experience. I believe or I want to believe (you know—all the variations) that it started out in some milder form and gradually worked its way up to the invasive version I'm describing here. There are stages. Maybe the first time he wanted to rest we did rest, and maybe I, unused to the workout, also wanted to rest. It's easy, from here, to map out the moves it would have taken, but I don't know how long it took to go from sitting down to sitting beside each other to sitting closer and then, as she is now, the child in this portrait or rather sketch, sitting on his lap. As he insisted. If it had started out as it ended up, I want to assert, I wouldn't have … I would never have: I want to protest. If it had started like that I would never have learned to say *touché*, I wouldn't know the little I do know about this sport or art.

Although I never returned to it, never even thought of taking a lesson, I knew I'd loved fencing: loved the clash of the blades and combination of force and strategy, loved the excitement of scoring a hit, "a veritable hit," the padded tip of the foil moving as if magnetized toward the invisible (or was it—it comes back dimly—marked?) heart of the white jacket. I haven't looked at the clothing or paraphernalia since, though the foil followed me around for awhile, sitting on shelves in various closets, until it was sold, maybe back to Mr. Jerome, now I think of it: who else could my parents have found to … That's the point at which everything stops, as I write this, and where I feel lost, unable to articulate anything sensible about the way in which a surface of normality remained almost completely untroubled by a situation that left so much deep confusion 'in its wake,' as we say. I have to do better than that.

In a corner of the big room, to the wonderful sliding clash of steel on steel which is a sound I had forgotten, I lunge into emptiness, I parry the air, I watch from behind the tight, close and slightly darkened area of the mask the end, the bouton (now they are electrified, then, or so I recall, they were just a wad of tape), of the foil as I pierce the bright wide open space of my reach. I have long arms and legs: that can be an advantage. You could do épée, my colleague remarks, where there is no part of the body that is off limits … Though there is only a layer of wire mesh between us, I feel as if he cannot see my face (I am invisible, invincible), and yet I turn away at that.

At some point … at what point? How long did it take? Can we go by the words that come back: *balestra*, *coulé*, *en garde*, oh, "en garde"—I had forgotten that: he used the French, the language I would come (later and elsewhere) to learn and love—how long to get to the *coup passé*, how far past *feinte*? At some point the lessons were so ruptured by his increasingly urgent and intimate explorations of my body I couldn't go on. In some way, and I have no recollection of the dumb words I used but they would've been, I imagine, the usual ones for this situation, the ones the children say to the psychologists and the psychologists, showing the clumsy, vivid drawings at the trial, quote, something flat: "I didn't like …," or some such phrase. There was no trial, in fact there was no follow-up, really, that I knew of, aside from my taunts on that memorable afternoon of my boldness. Maybe I didn't really make it clear to my parents, maybe I'd waited too long to speak. I knew I didn't like what was happening, but I'd known for some time that I didn't like it. But I also knew I was (I don't think he ever had to say anything about it) in his debt: I knew the lessons couldn't be free, I knew there was some cost and (I hate writing this) I was prepared to bear it—up to a point. I don't think I said that to my parents: that they were taking care of me was in some part a myth, but I was as eager as anyone to protect us all from the truth. I'm fairly sure I didn't ever say "I thought I could pay for …"—but they would've known on some level what it meant, my long (how long?) silence? I thought I could pay—but then I couldn't. Even the memory of telling my mother—the memory of bringing the incident to a close—is a relief. I recall that we were in the kitchen but not what I said. I am sure my mother was shocked and upset and my stepfather, when she told him, was angry, but as my mother was mostly shocked and upset and my stepfather was usually angry I may be making that up. I think my stepfather took his anger over to Mr. Jerome's and that I was glad that he was going to say something, something I couldn't, though I was also nervous and felt (this comes back) ashamed. But I don't know what was said and the anger he took past the hedge and into the other yard came back with him, without any visible effect. It would be decades before I saw clearly how constant and useless my parents' emotions were— but I am probably not lying if I say that at that point I might have already suspected a certain lack of weight. Mr. Jerome remained our neighbor for another couple of years, until we moved. My last vivid image of him is as seen through the picture window of our dining room, when we were at lunch. We had a guest staying with us whose dog was outside and off the leash, and, in the lovely soft Southern California light, Mr. Jerome appears, carrying a shovel loaded with dog shit, which he ostentatiously dumps into our yard. That's it. His eyes might have been blue.

And he was a natty dresser—I'd forgotten that. A silk scarf at the withered throat, perhaps. "The story leads to other stories," says the friend who's just published a fine and rather disturbing memoir, to whom, now, others open their hearts. "And then what," she wonders, with a certain impatience.

The initial charge, for the gear, will be $190.00 or so (the Fencing Club has an arrangement with "Blue Gauntlet"), though there may be some difficulty about the foil, as I want what I recall having then: a "Belgian grip." "We don't," one of the coaches says stiffly, "usually let beginners start out with a Belgian grip," which of course makes me want it more. I find the stance, my left arm raised beside my masked head, I begin to advance and (as the footwork, a dense combination of shuffle and jump, comes back) I lunge, I recover, I retreat. They were private lessons. The dues at the club are $50.00 a month: low, the head coach informs me, for a martial art. I am a full Professor, I don't say that except to myself, by which I mean to say this: I can afford it. As I think of what all it is I am saying as I say that it makes me a bit more sympathetic with the aspect of *Walden* that drove me nuts at first: the author's persnickety lists of what he spent and his gloating over how much (for how little he'd spent) he'd got. *I can afford it*, are words which, when meant (when true), must be lovely in any language.

And then what? There's something about the act of speaking after such a long silence: the memories seem lighter, somehow, the whole story slightly less serious. *Are you sure I never told you?* But I can't find, yet, a stopping place. It could have been better not to be attractive is a thought that will come, a stupid feeling maybe, hardly a thought. An old way of trying to find a sense of control in the outcome: if it were my fault there would be something I could do? (In my twenties, overwhelmed by attention, I put on some weight—it got me a respite.) Such an awful thing: this blaming, this heavy guilt. Better the hand of any creep, I almost want to say, than the touch of my own mind, with its restless wish to punish and blame, with its endless refrain: *your mistake, your fault.* I want them separate and they are not separate: the touch and the mind and heart that make what they will or can or must and maybe should not of that touch. The touch, and the response: transformative. Intimacy is magic … somewhere along the way I learned to shut myself off, to disappear in an embrace, first to endure a caress I did not enjoy, and then to fake enjoyment. Even what was true, what did matter, the actual and amazing pleasures, the real lovers, never stopped feeling dangerous. My heart races, my heart pounds, you thrill me: so go the clichés and the song lyrics. He feels her heart beating as he draws her near, her: in the Romance, the heroine, who always (at first) resists. Maybe fear is always some part of it? I think you would say, or maybe you would want to say, it doesn't have to be like that.

Dreams, after writing this (after some number of drafts) of moving through the world with the mask on: seeing everything through that slightly dimming mesh, from within a private space in which I feel safe—but, of course, isolated. "It doesn't ever quite let its defenses down," a reader remarked of this essay: "I get how horrible it was but I don't really get it." If I try to come closer the feeling that comes up first is an immense weariness: the resignation of a body long subdued to the dictates of a will. I don't want to do this. Heat of skin, prickle of mustache, a tongue, I'd forgotten, prying at my tight lips. Did I shut my eyes? Did he shut his? I could have said no, I could have said *no* sooner. I don't want to hear any excuses. The stark light and the cadence of the return to another relationship, because (in a moment) we will stand up (in a moment, in another moment) (if I can get through this), he will show me another complicated move, and I will practice it until I have it right. And I will be grateful for his praise of my skill, such as it is.

When I got this down, as we say, when I stopped writing and stepped away from the piece, feeling it was mostly in place … what came to me was a sudden belated horror at my compromised relationships with some of my former (oh yes "former," so carefully *former*—this was long ago, this was when I first started teaching, I want to try to explain this) students. I want to sound tough: I wrote "my former (okay-the-grades-are-in-now-we-can-fuck) students." I want to make it sound worse than it was? I don't want to write it down but if I do it has to be as bad as I can make it—as if it's crucial that I be the worst person I know. I fell in love, and then I let myself be seduced, and then later almost seduced and when I finally said (to myself) *no more of that*, I skidded into the turn, sleeping with my students' ex-boyfriends and soon-to-be-ex-girlfriends before it all came to a halt. I need to apologize—though this, *I'm sorry*, is only a start. "Nothing was given me of which I have not rendered some account," Thoreau writes, early in the book. And then, later: "The volatile truth of our words should continually betray the inadequacy of the residual statement." This *Walden* comes boxed in faded teal cloth, it has engravings by Thomas W. Nason: the

publication date is 1939. "I know no man worse than myself."
After 1939 most of the world can say if not *I know a man* then *I know* of *a man worse than myself*. The key, I think, for Thoreau, is the preposition: that is, its absence. To know the other (best and worst) in life and then within oneself, through oneself (that close) is to exist in that day, that Spring day, that present, which "is a truce to vice." Someone put it all in storage, the beautiful Heritage Press editions and well-thumbed copies of *Playboy* and *Hustler*, along with the flatware, and died without telling anyone how to take care of it, and so it comes back out: into the world. The lessons were real: there is a closely enfolded, inextricable, joy and sorrow I shall never be able to separate in that realization. "I left the woods for as good a reason as I went there," Thoreau says, winding up his account. I'm glad I told you. Usually what ends things for me is a failure of trust.

Structured Intervention / "fluency strategy"
(Miss Havisham Effect)

"A *point* is a particular moment in which an event tightens, from which it must in some ways be replayed, as if it returned under a displaced, modified, form, obliging you to 'redeclare' … It is necessary to say again, 'I accept this chance, I desire it, I take it on'." (Alain Badiou, *Eloge de l'amour*)

"My father's family name being …" I sit quietly beside you, as the script instructs, in a location in which we will not be disturbed. We read together, aloud, and when you feel that you can go on without me you tap the back of my hand, like this.

"What do I touch?"

Enter through a side door, the main way chained shut, always too late. Cold weight of steel across the great door now, where hope came in (but it was false) and went out. Follow a candle through halls no sunlight reaches, to be abandoned there (the flame sways as she turns away, your scornful guide, the little glow moves off as the girl is backlit, a thin line of fire traced around her golden hair and fresh skin, so the hand she holds up to guard the light seems to be itself the source of the light as she turns away) and, turning back to the shut door, knock.

In my mind the abruptly broken off chords of the wedding march, the tune that won't stop starting only to stop and stop and stop; I hear a jangled note abruptly crashing into dissonance, and I hear or imagine I hear the pitying, shocked, or excited gasps. How many of the guests (expressing shock and pity) secretly congratulated themselves on being there for—what could make a better story?—a marriage that never came off ...

The intention is to present reality "in a receivable way." They drag her spitting and shrieking into daylight and she passes out, falling down in the dust at the edge of the road. "It's okay," the counselor says, with a smile that oozes *understanding*, as they strap her onto the gurney, "nobody wants to get better, not at first."

It's a laugh or was once. You, you, you, protagonist, your name a caught seed in the teeth, cut word, abrupt, you advance along lines others plot for you and you, you mistake for good luck.

The _____ is waiting near the edge of the overgrown garden, by the rusted gate.

Moving on or rather forward means to get back to the *work* of getting married or trying to get married, yes? Oh, there's some lip service to the idea that I can be happy and fulfilled "all by myself" but in fact you expect to see me fall in love again soon: you will be concerned if I don't date someone, if I remain single, as if you knew (though you never say this) that if I remain on my own I will discover I don't really matter, don't really count ... I will be invited to fewer parties, wait longer to be served in stores, and the doctor you call—when I'm ill—may actually say, "Well, she's had a good life." Meaning, *enough*.

Open-ended, non-judgmental questions or statements of feeling are best: "Hello _____, I want you to know how sorry I am for your loss. How are you doing?"

This barred gate, you get there through numbers, numbness— you get me? Lies or at least silence. "But nothing more." Out on the marshes or meshes you met ...—forget that part. Sometimes you just have to hold onto whatever it is you've got. Production halts.

Well. "You": what *is* that? "We were only trying to help"?

The dirty whiteness of the room, the pale yellowing blankness of so much of what you see when you enter, makes a sort of vague, pale mist. The figure posed before the glass would not even seem feminine were it not for the long white hair and fancy dress. Turning at your entrance she seems to break a few silvery lines of web, as if she was being woven into her reflection, spun slowly into the cocoon of her own regard. Wasn't she, isn't she? Doesn't the glance always come back?

"'Your heart.'" My heart ...

The first meeting goes well enough: objectives are clear and the emotional investment of the participants in the outcome is apparent.

"I don't wish to make a display of my feelings, but ..."

I hear the timid knock again on the door of the one who came gently to break the bad news and I hear the click of the latch as I shut the door, turning the key. I cross the room and I am not crying: I don't cry. I pick up the clock, this is the first thing I do, and I throw it on the floor. Time stops. There. *He knew*, I will say later, *how I take care of myself.*

The noun is *Jilt*, the form of the verb is "to jilt." Conjugate, conjugal. "I hope you have someone to keep you warm," he said, or "to warm you." The diagnosis is "Complicated Grief," "previously known as chronic, pathological or traumatic grief."

It's almost instantaneous, the understanding that there is nothing beyond this moment and that everything needs to stop; the rest is preparation for stasis, worship of the foreclosed event.

The ragged dust-blackened foot of her stocking slides up to reveal one filthy scaling heel. The fragile lace of the dress has cracked, bits of stiff fabric sift down like snowflakes or dandruff as she shifts in the hard fold-out chair, picking at the frayed edges of her grayish satin underskirt, looking at the floor or the wall or ... anywhere but at us.

So, uhm, *reframing* "I will never get married" turns it into "I want to get married"? *I* want?

Frustrated but firm, keyed up, your expressions, self-righteous and excited: you are enjoying your power, perhaps? The power of the artist? To intervene, to revise or restructure *take under pencil came forgive*: like that? To change the syntax? Only, of course, your work is in the service of sense—and mine is not (as far as you can see). You see what you are doing as getting the story "back on track": correcting an aberration, resetting a dislocation, revising a bizarre mistake. But you are always free (you have made this clear enough!) to not even bother to read the alternate versions I present.

The visage a troubled blank, a circle of paper worn by the scrubbing out of endless wrong answers. The "permanent" is here reduced to a degree of tightness or inflexibility, uneasy traces of denied life.

Our voices are joined as my finger moves across and down the page: "When you say you love me, I know what you mean, as a form of words …" And then the pressure on my hand, and, "Boot nuh-thing mohr," as sounded out.

He wouldn't marry me, wasn't thinking of marrying me, although he wanted, so he said, *nothing more than to be married* … Well, he put it like this: "I want the white picket fence." I knew that let me out.

A text letter by letter tugged from an orifice dry as the paper itself; read by the guttering end of a greasy light. Vaginal *atrophy*? Really? Is there a correspondent …

Talking about it, sitting in groups. Weekly meetings of professional or upper middle-class women who each stood up in turn to confess, "My name is _____ and I'm … single … unmarried … a spinster," or (the stronger ones) "a jilt."

"But she was a MESS, I mean, her life was a total mess, and she was laying all this really heavy shit on me, like I'd have to go out and 'break hearts' (that was her phrase) FOR her or something. Hurt other people. And I was getting all twisted up inside 'cause it seemed like I couldn't take the risk of loving anyone, 'cause love was ... only a game, but ... a dangerous game ... too dangerous ..."

And so it stops, and starts again in order to stop, just ... here. (What do I touch?)

No one is to mention time to me now: *I have nothing to do with the days of the weak.* At night I pace the length of the dust-encrusted, spider-charged table set with the rotting feast or else I make up strange dances in the dimming mirrors, moaning to myself. My arms around an invisible partner, I waltz, murmuring reassuring or flirtatious nothings, until I collapse. Sometimes I smear my face with clay or cream and, wearing nothing but that heavy blank mask, totter nude across the long table assuming suggestive poses above each setting. Or else I might move from chair to chair, talking and laughing in imitation of each imagined guest. I am both the spectacle and the whole audience, each strained smile and stammered set of congratulations; I pause at each place long enough to lift a glass to myself, to us ... Our happiness. Some nights the toasts are explicit to the point of pornography, some nights they are so tender and heartfelt I can barely whisper these speeches I believe I might have heard on that day (if you hadn't left ...) and ... and I try to weep.

When you halt over some new configuration of tangled letters or badly mispronounce a word I join my voice to yours, and we go on together until I feel the gentle pressure of your hand on this glove of loose, yellowing, age-spotted flesh.

But if I'd slept with him, he claimed, he might've left her for me, might have wanted to be with me instead of her, might have thought or felt he had to "commit" to me at that point. Where *slept with* means *fucked*.

I have identified that s/he is feeling very ashamed about what happened, and feels very isolated and alone.

Way back where it started you supplied a file for someone else's chain—before you forged your own—you brought a picnic to someone making a break for it. In fear of your life. The phonemes catch, break up, as you sound out who you are, what it is you can say of it, to be inserted as subject in this unfinished sentence. Well it's this longing to grasp what we think is the source of our joy that we share, isn't it? To make the eternal from a chance? "Boy?" I speak ("'Boy'") from some distance.

The coffee is lousy because that is the cliché and because the cliché is the necessary dose of reality, or "realism," meaning we ground ourselves in the real by way of these touchstones more plausible than accurate. Lukewarm brew in its Styrofoam container: inky and sour as my own thoughts.

"Broken."

Then silence, and after a moment we go on again together, "… you touch nothing there."

It's a candle in a long dark corridor, this image of my grief that is my remembered grief. Little glow sucked after, entreating, the vanished gust.

Each time you come in it's yet another woman wearing the decaying outfit, speaking these lines, reading from the letter he left her with (a tissue of clichés meant mostly to shore up his own feeling of self-importance): various ages, races, and nationalities, these women, enraged, disgusted, or laughing: they model a number of reactions to his decision to leave her (please, "to jilt"!), alike only in their willingness to pause there, to spend time in this space of sorrow and shame they are transforming, *because* they are willing to dwell in this moment or, as you'd say, "obsess."

"You know …, sometimes when people have experienced a sudden lose (*sic*) and feel as you do, they think about suicide. Is this something you have thought about?"

Some nights I stay up for hours, cruising an on-line dating service, discarding "matches," improving my profile, enticing admiration I disdain or discard: proving I can still *break hearts*.

And you are "armed" (such is the verb choice) with "factual, non-judgmental data."

The funky room where they meet is always somewhere a little askew, and ugly. Not the church but the basement of the church, you know ("Where does a masochist live? / In a basement"), the light too bright or dim, the air scented by unwashed bodies, stale pastries, coffee boiled too long, and undisturbed dust, as if to insist that the lives to which we must return, when we "get better," our illusions stripped away, are *completely devoid of charm*," blasted by bad choices and neglect.

"I couldn't really connect with anyone, you know? Like, if I even thought about it I could feel her there again, brrrrr: the slither of chill gems along my neck as she tried each ornament out; I could hear her eager laugh and see that hungry look. 'Never let a man get in the way of your career'—never let never let never let . . . Then her breathless urgent gasp: 'Break their hearts!' "

Whenever appropriate or feasible, participants were encouraged to choose condom-related goals.

"What do you mean, 'I'll show them'?"

"What have I done!" "When she first came in I meant to save her from misery like mine." "Take the pencil and write under my name, 'I forgive her'!"

"What have I . . . !" "When first . . . I meant to save . . . from misery like . . ." "Take . . ." ". . . Have I . . . !" "When she . . . to . . ." "Take . . . my name . . . !" "What I meant . . . misery . . . !" "Have . . . I . . . meant to . . . write . . ."

"I hope you have someone to warm you," he said, meaningfully, by way of goodbye (while his wife was in the bathroom) . . .

You see me *taking steps on the road to recovery*? Like, what? Reading *He's Just Not That Into You*, maybe, in a women's book club? Cutting and dying my hair? Dieting? Taking a Pilates class? Signing up at an on-line dating site? Making a list of what I want in a man? Let's see ... could he just not be a complete jackass?!

I pictured him then as if in a drawing done by a child, you know: a stick figure holding the hand of another stick figure, smaller stick figures off to the side, the sun a scrawl of yellow, the tree a scribble of green, the house a simple box with an upside down "V" for a roof. All of this behind the regular vertical lines that alert us to the presence of the suburban border. Property rights.

"Vanity of sorrow ..."

Production halts, you move past the stilled signs, your password the name of a man we can't admit. Get to it. The rusted gate, the windows blocked up or barred, the walls of "dismal" brick, a lot of empty barrels what's left of a long gone pleasure: a sparkling brew, golden as urine or late sunlight, a drink that once quenched the harsh word and the sweet, flowing down long-vanished throats as if to seek the source of that echoing laugh.

" 'What do I touch?' / You're *hurt*."

A story emerges where the story we were supposed to hear halts: from a narrative interrupted another narrative appears, apparently without development, or the development is cyclic, oblique.

Our voices sliding across the text, phoneme by phoneme, joined and distinct, this constant experience of difference and shared focus, and then the moments in which you continue alone, and my silent sounding out of the space you cross without me, with my love.

Admitted to a house one of whose names means *Enough*.

This client-centered counseling intervention had the following aims: increase participants' perception of personal risk, support participant initiated changes, and focus on small, achievable steps toward reducing personal risks.

" 'Broken!' "

"Okay … I understand. You see no hope. But I do. You need to come with me right now." (My voice is compassionate, but firm.)

Torch Song

(Prose is a Prose is a Prose)

"That's the way fire does, it don't have no rules on it"
(Anonymous firefighter, speaking of the progress of the Hayman fire, Colorado, 2002)

"I think her words were, 'You're going to be really mad at me.' I don't think I was mad at her, I was just more shocked and saddened." (Forest Service Ranger Sara Mayben, describing former Forest Service Technician Terry Barton's admission of responsibility for the Hayman fire)

Story #1: She smelled smoke and discovered fire.

Proverb: *Where there's smoke there's fire.*

Perverbs
      (*homage to Harry Mathews*)
All roads lead to fire
Where there's smoke there's a way
A rolling stone gathers no fire
Smoke waits for no man
The road to hell is paved with fire
A match in the sand is worth two above the timber line
When the cat's away there's fire
What goes up must …
                  in flames

It Speaks: A failure of belief is often figured as a problem of incorporation: *No one would swallow that*, we say, or, "it just doesn't smell right." It *stinks*. Sometimes that's as close as we can get to it. To "burn" is also to deceive. Given the distance and the wind direction … —this scent of smoke (clinging to cloth and skin, tangled in hair) vanishes into air we insist is "thin." As any excuse.

Story #1a (her own words): "I saw the fire and tried to put it out."

Hayman Fire "at a glance" (updated from the *Coloradoan*, June 21, 2002)
Size: 138,000 acres
Evacuations: 8,200
Damage: 133 homes destroyed.
On scene: 2,508 personnel.
Fatalities: 6
Cost: $39 million.

Discussion Topic, Technologies and Gestures: In a transparent sentence the subject sees and comes to knowledge and then action, though here the imbalance of verbs as well as the syntax (note the distance of the "I" from that final, failed effort: "I saw the fire and tried to put it out") alerts us to the speaker's sense of powerlessness. Before she got there, the fire, before anything— before the speech it sparks, or the writing she'll later claim started it—"kindled by a person unknown." "I saw the fire": "I" is a shifter. Do you see her seeing (a face at the edge of the frame, registering—in slightly too-lurid color—shock and increasing dismay) or do you see yourself in her place? "[A]nd tried to put it out." "I … tried." Repeat at least 2,500 times.

Re: Vision: "Tirelessly the process of thinking makes new beginnings, returning in a roundabout way to its original object." (Walter Benjamin, *The Origin of the German Tragic Drama*) "Mosaic": the term for the varied and broken patterns a fire traces, comprehending a landscape, "burning at different intensities in different places and … burning different places in different years." (Margaret Fuller: *Forest Fires*)

Story #2: "She reported that she looked at a letter that she had received that morning from her estranged husband. She became angry and upset and tried to get rid of the letter." (Court document.)

Advice from a fiction writer (dead): "You've got to sell your heart, your strongest reactions, not the little minor things that only touch you lightly … This is especially true when you begin to write, when you have not yet developed the tricks of interesting people on paper, when you have none of the technique which it takes time to learn. When, in short, you have only your emotions to sell." (F. Scott Fitzgerald)

(Back) Story #2a: At one point we're told that our heroine's two teenage daughters put a letter of their father's into their mother's day pack before she went off to work. Their goal, *repairing the marriage*; her job, *protecting the wilderness*.

Re: Vision: A woman enters a forest with a letter. The letter, a love letter, never mentions the forest but some people can look at a stand of trees and see nothing but paper. The sweet, rank, cloying stench of the pulp mill fills the air a thousand miles from here. Some people can look at a line of words and see nothing but reference—or the lack of it—most of the sentence seems like a by-product, a way to get there. The defendant declared she "stayed with the burning letter until it had burned completely." Most people, visiting our national parks, never go more than 250 feet away from their cars.

Back draft: *"Darling I can't live without you,"* etc. Before they fold the letter into their mother's day pack, the girls read the trite phrases over to each other in awed, hushed whispers punctuated by—on the part of the youngest—fits of uncomfortable giggles. In short they read it like teenage girls. They *are* teenage girls: we know what that means.

Questions for further study: *What does that mean?*
Questions for further study: Are you thinking here of the book or the movie, the original or the remake of *The Parent Trap*?
Questions for further study: How did the girls get their hands on the letter?
Questions for further study: Do you find these "characters" "sympathetic"?
Questions for further study: *What does that mean?*

And the Word *Was* Light: Reread Jacques Lacan on Edgar Allen Poe's story "The Purloined Letter"? Reread Poe: the letter is set out in plain sight so it can't be seen; the letter must be recovered and can't be read, ever; the letter is replaced by another letter which *can* be read: but the words are not the words of the letter's author. Reread Walter Benjamin ("The reader warms his shivering life with a death he reads about": "The Story Teller"). "[S]he was so upset after reading the letter that she burned it inside a campfire ring but it escaped, accidentally igniting Colorado's largest wildfire." (*Coloradoan* [6/22/02].)

Questions for further study: What work is "accidentally" doing in the above sentence? And then, "largest"?
Questions for further study: In the phrase "burned it … but it escaped" is the pronoun's reference secure?

Re: Vision: As if made for a made-for-TV-movie the already tired scene played over and over: "She was so upset," etc. (Question: How upset do you need to be to burn 138,000 acres?) The print is grainy. Did you see her, "in your mind's eye," with matches, crying so her hand shook too much to strike a light at first? Or do you picture her standing there, resolute, raising a lighter aloft like a concert-goer during the known-by-heart encore? "The only thing that is different from one time to another is what is seen and what is seen depends upon how everybody is doing everything," Gertrude Stein repeats ("Composition As Explanation"). The Russian filmmaker Andrey Tarkovsky dies in exile, his countrymen having refused his vision, even now some people say of his movies that there's not enough story there. In *The Mirror* a drenched woman appears in the charred room of a gone house, a dream or memory, haunting the narrator. *Homage*, as if the word had a home in it. All the elements the filmmaker loved and lovingly reassembled are here: the woman, the forest, the tears … a letter on fire.

Out-Takes, or **Everybody's Ex** (June 21, 2002): The stuff of the event burns so fast—there's no time to establish or absorb any single story, or to see a previous version be fully replaced by another, so that all the possible truths seem still to be in play, though only able uneasily to acknowledge each other. Remember the zero story? Something about a car spotted fleeing the scene. Was a male figure mentioned or did I make that up? Some guy … —boiling water for coffee, or noodles, or? Ready in an instant, as if he were himself a reconstituted soup mix, this character: the beer in his hand, the car radio blaring "Smoke on the Water," the story he tells himself in half-phrases, "Shit, she used to love it here …"—the way he roughly brushes at his eyes with the back of his fist, and tosses his cigarette butt at the campfire pit—"ah, goddamn it …"

Notes on craft (fiction): A false line of dialogue can ruin an entire scene.

Notes on craft (forestry): Old burns tend to stop fires.

Story #2b ("What's this paper doing here?"): Our heroine pulls her ex-husband's letter from her pack, alone in the forest, and breaks down, deciding to burn it at once, which we are meant to 'understand' or to be understanding about—although she is in fact on duty, in her role as a Forest Service Technician, enforcing a ban on fires, in her first, probationary, year.

It Speaks: A failure of understanding is often figured as a failure of grasp. We say "I don't get it." We say, "The meaning completely escaped her." Anne Carson remarks Paul Celan's idea of language as net or grillwork—*Sprachgitter*—in whose limits and meshes we are "cleanse[d] of the illusion that we could talk." (*Economy of the Unlost* 33)

Story #3 (tests on the debris): Her husband "told investigators he never wrote her a letter. Prosecutors also said there was no evidence of burned paper at the scene, but they are still conducting tests on the debris."

Discussion Topic: Technologies and Gestures (or, The Company Bar-B-Q): Unquestioned understanding: of course you burn a *love* letter (literary precedents: *The Wings of the Dove,* etc.) (Question: *was* that a love letter?), but—even as we imagine the tender words (had tears splotched the paper?) turning to ash—a question occurs. What if, as is so likely now, the letter was written on a computer? (Reread Benjamin, "The Work of Art in the Age of Mechanical Reproduction" etc.) Oh, but surely not a *love* letter?! Our desire to allot specific technologies a certain range of emotional gestures is itself worth a paper. Discuss the differences in texture-of-event between burning a love letter and shredding documents. Why *don't* we shred love letters? Or do we? If it had turned out that Ollie North and Fawn Hall had sat up late burning the Iran-Contra evidence together would we think they were in love? If it turned out that accountants at Arthur Anderson *burned* the proof of their relationship with Enron? What if the pages were used to help the coals catch beneath the stiff suckling pig on the turning spit, as full of righteous indignation as any accused executive?

Q. What would you save from a house on fire?
A. The fire (Jean Cocteau)

Backdraft: For days we'd been reading, beneath the dry (!) news reports, the easy clichés this letter would have had to include, a fire beginning "I love you"; a fire beginning, "I want to start over." The tears in the reader's eyes give the air a heat shimmer. Okay. Now you have two hours to go back in and bring out everything you want to save forever. *As is so often the case, the words had a powerful effect, though not the one intended by their author!*

What We Talk About When We Talk About Creative Writing: In those contemporary stories which still function, despite appearances, as instruction manuals for if not *good* then at least *better* behavior, our heroine brusquely crumples the letter, thinks for a minute, unfolds it again and, putting the offending document on the seat beside her, drives home. If she doesn't have the almost requisite fender bender (late 20th century epiphany territory: a chance for some sudden intersubjectivity and necessary soul searching), she arrives home, lowers the blinds, pours herself a drink and plays something like "Smoke Gets In Your Eyes" over and over. It's as if what she's read has seared itself into her memory, the rhythm of those terse sentences with their focus on physical details, e.g.: The little clunk of ice against the glass made a cool noise that soothed her.

Advice from the tribe's piece of tale: "Sometimes trying to rekindle an old flame works, but frequently the best advice we can give a woman who thinks she's still in love with her ex is *Next!*" (*The Rules II* 25)

Story #2c: During the trial one of Barton's daughters will testify that her mother was following the advice of a psychologist, who'd told her to write her feelings down in a letter—and then to burn it.

The Plea: Innocent
The Sentence: overturned.
The Sentence: *an opportunity to demonstrate remorse.*
The Sentence: "We have yet to take our thinking about fiction to the level of the sentence." (Kass Fleisher)

Story #4: "In the custody," as Maurice Blanchot puts it, "of the third person," a report lists our protagonist's age (38) in the sentence describing her as "dry-eyed as she entered the plea." And continues, "But after Thursday's hearing got under way, she wiped away tears and reached for a tissue as one witness, U.S. Forest service special agent Brenda Schultz, said it appeared [the defendant] had moved rocks from a campfire to allow the fire to escape and ignite surrounding brush." (*Coloradoan*)

Advice from a poet (dead): "No tears for the writer, no tears for the reader." (Robert Frost)

Discussion Topic, Gestures and Technologies: An acid trip allowed Anais Nin to discover that women weep because "IT IS THE QUICKEST WAY TO REJOIN THE OCEAN." Loyola's journal traced his spiritual progress by recording his degree of responsiveness to the act of worship, noting the absence or presence, while praying, of tears. Recall and discuss instances (from life or literature) in which this bodily function marks a "dissolve" between public (exterior) and private (interior). In your own experience, is this a gender-specific technology? In the report above, why is the defendant crying? What do tears stand for here?

Questions for further study: What are the social benefits of a legible body or a body perceived as legible? What costs might be involved in the production of such bodies, both presently and in the future? Who pays and how?

Story #4a? Or 5?: She dreams of being a fire inspector, a debris-sifter, one of the experts called in after the whole thing's over. She can tell you everything that happened there, and in what order: she can tell you the whole story. Just one glance and she knows how this one began. She shakes her head. We can't see her eyes behind the sunglasses but her brow is furrowed and her lips are firmly pressed together. "You see what I see?" she asks, but we never do, not ever, not until she tells us what to see. She shakes the evidence into a carefully labeled plastic bag as we notice the tan line on her left hand's ringless third finger.

The Hearing: "I feel good. It's done," she'll say (in 2008), looking relaxed at the hearing; she'll say she doesn't want *forgiveness*—she just wants us (all) "to move on."

The State: "No one spoke on behalf of the state."

Debris or Not Debris: "It was expressing John's feelings for Terry that he loved her and wanted to get back together with her …" (Connie Work, family friend). These blank skies and astonishing, romantic sunsets. Static in the background heavily amplified to stand for the sound of the fire. Heavily over-grown forests, residential construction in so called "red areas," an increase in the population of wood-eating beetles, and almost no snowpack: *Now you're getting warmer.* A friend—out west for the (canceled) family vacation—stays until the fire is over, in order to go through the ashes with his parents, looking at what his grandparents (who built the cabin) can't bear to see. Some people would say there's nothing to see here: this blackened rubble full of strange shapes it takes hard observation and sessions of guessing to remember, to place, to recall the use of, to restore to meaning. But that thin line of lead might be a pencil, those shards of metal the exploded lamp, maybe. What's left of the mirrors and windows these twisted, gleaming, stopped flows of melted glass: these frozen tears. "Fuck it," the poet's tattoo says, "burn everything." The problem of breathing in this atmosphere.

Questions for further study: Do you think we could just start over?

Laura **Mullen** is the author of seven previous books, including *Dark Archive*, *Subject*, *After I Was Dead*, and *The Surface*, which was a National Poetry Series selection. Her poems are included in *Postmodern American Poetry*, *American Hybrid*, and *I'll Drown My Book: Conceptual Writing by Women*, among other anthologies. The composer Jason Eckardt's setting of her poem "The Distance (This)" was released as *Undersong* by Mode Records in 2011, and a collaboration with the composer Nathan Davis was premiered by the La Jolla Symphony and Chorus in 2014. Mullen's honors and awards include fellowships from the National Endowment for the Arts, the Rona Jaffe Foundation, and the MacDowell Colony. She is the McElveen Professor in English and Director of Creative Writing at Louisiana State University.